THE STORY
OF
HANDWRITING

by Alfred Fairbank
A HANDWRITING MANUAL

by Alfred Fairbank and Berthold Wolpe
RENAISSANCE HANDWRITING:
An Anthology of Italic Scripts

miles duobus aut tribus comitatus. quom ipsum cognouisset. in ve
stibulum quoddam protraxit. incipientem iam se ictu recipere.

bi quum Zopirus ceruicem incisurus gladium eduxisset ita
torue respexit eum pyrrhus: ut illum ad tremorem prae metu
compelleret. Nec recte sed ad os et mentum ceruicem secaret.
iam res pluribus nota erat: quom Alcyoneus Antigoni filius

A. PLUTARCH. Pyrrhus's Last Fight in the Market-place of Argos. Fifteenth century.
British Museum (Add. MS. 22318).

THE STORY
OF
HANDWRITING

Origins and Development

ALFRED J
FAIRBANK

Watson-Guptill Publications
New York

First published in 1970
by Faber and Faber Limited
24 Russell Square, London, W.C.1
Published in 1970
by Watson-Guptill Publications
165 West 46 Street, New York, N.Y. 10036
Library of Congress
Catalog Card Number: 77–84820

For Richard, Anna and Ruth

Acknowledgements

Grateful acknowledgements for permission to use copyright material or for assistance is made as follows: to the Director of the British Museum, the Keeper of Western Manuscripts, Bodleian Library, the Deputy Keeper of the Public Record Office, the Vice-prefect of the Biblioteca Apostolica Vaticana, the Conservateur du Département des Antiquités Orientales, The Louvre, the Director of the Biblioteca Medicea Laurenziana, Florence, the Superintendent of Antichità Dell' Etruria, Florence, the Director of the Stifsbibliothek, St. Gall, the Montpellier Medical Library, Montpellier, Professor I. J. Gelb and the University of Chicago Press, the Mansell Collection, Sir Isaac Pitman & Sons, Mr. Philip Hofer, Mrs. Chi Chou Watts, and Dr. Berthold L. Wolpe.

Contents

INTRODUCTION   *page* 17

THE BEGINNINGS OF WRITING   19

SUMERIAN WRITING   25

EGYPTIAN WRITING   27

CHINESE CALLIGRAPHY   29

THE DECIPHERING OF ANCIENT SCRIPTS   31

THE ALPHABET   37

THE LATIN SCRIPTS   41

THE CAROLINGIAN AND MEDIAEVAL SCRIPTS   45

THE SCRIPTS OF THE ITALIAN RENAISSANCE   47

COPPERPLATE WRITING   55

PRINT-SCRIPT   59

THE ITALIC HAND OF TODAY   61

FORMAL CALLIGRAPHY REVIVED   67

ILLUMINATED MANUSCRIPTS   71

LEGIBILITY   75

DIFFERENCES IN WRITING STYLES   77

MOTIONS AND SHAPES IN WRITING   80

PATTERN AND SPACING   82

PENS   85

INK   89

PAPER, VELLUM, AND PAPYRUS   92

THE TEACHING OF HANDWRITING   95

LEFT-HANDED WRITERS   100

SOME BOOKS TO CONSULT   102

INDEX   104

Illustrations

Plates in Colour

A. PLUTARCH. Fifteenth century. British Museum   *frontispiece*

B. THE BENEDICTIONAL OF ST. ETHELWOLD.
     Tenth century. British Museum   *facing page* 18

C. LA SOMME LE ROY. Illuminated by Honoré.
     Thirteenth century. British Museum   66

D. BOOK OF HOURS. Illuminated by the Master of
     Mary of Burgandy. Fifteenth century. Bodleian
     Library   71

Monochrome Plates

Plates 1–23 between pp. 32 and 33

1 & 2. Archaic clay tablets of the Jemdet Nasr type. About 2800 B.C.

3. Clay tablet from 'Atshana with envelope. Fifteenth century B.C.

4. Senena stele showing hieroglyphs. About 2350 B.C.

5. Hieratic script and illustration from *The Book of the Dead of Ani.*
Eighteenth Dynasty

6. Demotic script from the proceedings of a Court of Justice.
170 B.C.

7. Chinese oracle bone. About 1100 B.C.

8. Chinese signs for sheep and ocean with the water radical

9. Phaistos Disc. About 1700 B.C.

10. Moabite Stone of Mesha, King of Moab. Mid ninth century B.C.
11. Etruscan abecedarium. About 700 B.C.
12. Athenian *stoichedon* inscription. 408/7 B.C.
13. Inscription on the Trajan Column, Rome. A.D. 114
14. Square capitals with palimpsest. Fourth century A.D.
15. Rustic capitals. Fourth or fifth century A.D.
16. Roman cursive writing on papyrus. A.D. 522
17. Uncials. Eighth century A.D.
18. Half-uncials. Sixth century A.D.
19. Insular scripts of *The Lindisfarne Gospels*. Before 698 and the tenth century A.D.
20. Anglo-Saxon minuscules. Eighth century A.D.
21. Carolingian minuscules. Ninth century A.D.
22. Carolingian script of *The Ramsey Psalter*. Between A.D. 974 and 986
23. Late Carolingian script of N. Italy. Twelfth century A.D.

Plates 24–29 between pp. 48 and 49

24. Gothic textura script. About 1386
25. Humanistic (roman) script of Poggio Bracciolini. 1425
26. Humanistic cursive (italic) script of Niccolò Niccoli. ?1423
27. Roman script of Giacomo Curlo. Before 1458
28. Roman script of Alexander Antonii Simonis. 1477
29. Italic script of Antonio Tophio

Plates 30–38 between pp. 96 and 97

30. Italic script of an anonymous scribe at the Vatican Chancery. About 1490
31. Part of a Papal brief written by Arrighi. 27th August, 1519

32. Letter written by Elizabeth I when a princess to Thomas Seymour. 1548

33. Letter written by the Earl of Essex when aged nine. 1575

34. The 'Italique hande' from *A Booke Containing Divers Sortes of Hands* by Jean de Beauchesne. 1570

35. From *The Writing Schoolmaster or the Anatomy of Faire Writing* by John Davies of Hereford. 1663

36. Specimen scripts written by John Bowack for the Earl of Oxford. 31st December, 1712

37. Trial page written by William Morris. About 1875

38. *A New Handwriting for Teachers* by M. M. Bridges. 1898

Figures in text

1. Pictorial origin of some cuneiform signs   *page* 24

2. The Narmer Palette. About 2900 B.C.   28

3. The Rosetta Stone. 196 B.C.   34

4. The signs of the Early Phoenician alphabet. Eleventh century B.C.   36

5. The Praeneste Brooch. Seventh century B.C.   41

6a. Monogram of the Emperor Charlemagne   44

6b. The English secretary hand. Jean de Beauchesne. 1570   46

7. *La Operina* by Ludovico degli Arrighi. Rome, 1522   49

8. *Arte de escriver* by Francisco Lucas. Madrid, 1577   50

9. Portrait of Charles I by Joseph Goddard. ?1644   53

10. *The Universal Penman.* George Bickham. 1733–41   54

11. *The Theory and Practice of Handwriting* by J. Jackson. 1898   57

12. Italic alphabets for infants   *page* 58
13. Italic hand of Graily Hewitt. 1916   60
14-18. Examples from *Beacon Writing Books*   62–65
19. The 'foundational' hand written by Edward Johnston.
    1919   68
20. Broad pen roman alphabets and numerals   69
21. Demonstration of the *boustrophedon* system   74
22. From *Libellus valde doctus elegans*, etc., Zurich, 1549   79
23. Wood engraving by Noel Rooke   84
24. The manufacture of Chinese ink   88
25. Teaching the alphabet   99
26. Pen in left hand   101

Introduction

Inventions and discoveries were made in the remote past which are still important. The creation and evolution of speech and language are linked with the history of civilisation. How could mankind have achieved what it has without them? But speech in primitive conditions was limited to persons who were alive and actually present on a particular occasion, for the listener had to be within hearing. Today, speech by persons near and far is commonly conveyed by various technical devices and processes and even the voices of some who have died not long ago may be heard.

After the evolution of language another great stride forwards to the social conditions we enjoy was brought about by the invention of writing, and particularly by that of the alphabet with a limited number of signs sufficient, however, to represent the sounds of the language.

Through language and speech it has been possible to share with others our thoughts, ideas, and recollections, and to tell of happenings and situations, to narrate stories, and to keep records. By the invention of writing we are able to know something of the life of people even after the lapse of thousands of years. Writing is the father of printing.

The story of writing begins with the use of tools, materials, and methods now obsolete. Today we speak of handwriting, and also of calligraphy, and we then imply the use of pen and ink.

By some, handwriting may be thought to be just a dreary necessity we have to accept and to cope with. At its worst it fails to be legible, has little or no value, and is a nuisance. Happily, at its best it is a graphic craftsmanship, giving pleasure both to those who write and those who read, and a challenge to our skill and taste.

Obviously, legibility is of prime importance. The high degree of legibility we find in our printed books is due to standards of penmanship in Italy at the time printing was invented.

What is valued in the correspondence of our friends is the inevitable expression of personality. But the remarkable interest shown in the revival of italic handwriting during the last few years, both in this country and overseas, indicates that many persons have tired of graceless scribble and wish to write better.

B. The Benedictional of St. Ethelwold. A Bishop pronouncing a blessing.
Between A.D. 963 and 984. British Museum (Add. MS. 54180).

The Beginnings of Writing

The invention of writing seemed to ancient people to be so remarkable as to have a magical nature and to have been the gift of gods or the invention of their heroes. The gods Thoth and Isis were believed by the early Egyptians to have given them knowledge of writing, whilst other peoples claimed their own gods: the Babylonians, Nebo; the Greeks, Hermes; the Hindus, Brahma, etc. In England, an eighteenth-century writing-master, Joseph Champion, gave the credit either to God or to Adam. However, in *The Origin and Progress of Letters* published in 1773, the author, W. Massey, commented that he 'saw no necessity to suppose that our first parents should be capable of writing as soon as speaking; . . . for of what use could that have been at the first, when none but Adam and Eve, or a very few others were in the world?'. The father of Chinese writing, Ts'ang Chich, was thought to be so perceptive that he had been endowed with an extra pair of eyes.

Today we know by scholars' researches and discoveries that primitive man, living in caves 20,000 years or more before Christ, made paintings and carvings. Also that the beginnings of writing are in simple pictures. The prehistoric paintings of bulls, bison, horses and other animals of the Last Ice Age, on the walls of the caves of Altamira in Spain and Lascaux in France are impressive and powerful works of art we can admire and enjoy. Some of these paintings are thought to have served a purpose, aiding in the pursuit of beasts or as part of fertility rites, and were not made only to satisfy artistic urges and energy. Man's ability to depict was developed into two directions: towards art and thus to producing the superb sculptures of Greece and the paintings of the Italian Renaissance, but also by simple pictures and many stages to calligraphy.

We can and do communicate without the help of language or speech. There are, for example, the gestures, when no word needs to be spoken to convey meaning yet what we wish to express can also be conveyed by words: the agreeing nod, the welcoming smile, the shrug which tells of doubt. Communication can be by a simple picture or graphic sign irrespective of words. Two conventional and simplified signs commonly in use today are of an arrow-head or of a hand with a finger pointing which indicate a direction to be followed. That an arrow or a hand is represented does not mean we have to think of the words arrow or hand.

When trading began it was necessary to establish ownership. In Sumer, labels of clay were attached to objects as property marks and the marks were made by stamping clay with a seal. The later cylinder seal was rolled to make a rectangular design or a repeating pattern, and takes a place in the history of glyptic art. The mark of the seal was for personal indentity and represented a name and not a word to be associated with other words and to communicate (Plate 3). For this reason seals have not been held to be the actual beginning of writing. Today there is still the use of related signs of ownership and personal association such as the brand, the heraldic device, and the trade mark.

Some of the terms applicable to features found in the ancient writings may, as a convenience, be listed at this stage:

PICTOGRAMS. Simplified and conventionalized pictures of familiar objects, animals, etc., used as signs to represent what is depicted (picture-writing, pictography).

IDEOGRAMS. Word signs. An important development of picture-writing allowing the representation of ideas, actions, and associations. (The motorist is instructed by many ideograms as road-signs.)

PHONETIC WRITING. Each sign (phonogram) stands for a sound of the language. This principle leads on ultimately to the alphabet.

PHONEMES. The constituent sounds of a language: vowels, consonants, diphthongs.

DETERMINATIVES. Signs added to basic signs which help to fix meanings and remove ambiguities, but which are not pronounced. There are, however, also PHONETIC COMPLEMENTS, a form of determinative where the addition is to be pronounced.

TRANSITIONAL SCRIPTS. Scripts partly ideographic but partly phonetic.

LINEAR WRITING. Signs that have been developed from pictures but curves have changed to lines and are no longer pictorial. The Sumerian signs in Figure I are relevant. Some signs are simple geometric forms.

SYLLABARIES. These relate to writing of words of one or more syllables where signs represent syllables and not letters of an alphabet.

CURSIVE WRITING. Signs and styles of writing changed in form by everyday use and quickly executed construction.

ACROPHONIC PRINCIPLE. That signs derived their sound-values from the pronunciation of the initial of the word sign.

Picture-writing was used to help memory or to identify possessions or to make records of transactions, but its link with language was the key to civilisation. The pictograms were formalized so that they were recognized by persons other than the one making them. Moreover, they were changed in form by the materials and methods used, as well as by the cursive principle. Such drawings have been called shorthand-pictures, from being reductions to the merest indication of the things drawn. The picture of the head of an ox would serve just as well as a drawing of a whole ox, and be so simple that it could be drawn quickly and with little skill.

In simple pictography a circle might represent the word 'sun', but as an ideogram it might stand for 'bright', or 'light', or 'day' or 'time'. The ideographic system requires many signs: e.g. Chinese writing is ideographic and the literate Chinese need to be able to read and write thousands of different signs.

In the device we know as the rebus, pictures are used to represent words or syllables. A picture of an inn and a spire could be read as 'inspire', or a picture of a saw and the sea could read 'saucy'. It is even possible today to make sentences by the rebus principle: e.g. a sentence could be read from pictures of an eye, a can, a knot, a bee, a tray, a hymn (I cannot betray him).

A full system of writing was not achieved until the visual signs represented the sounds of the language, thus linking speech and writing. As these sounds are limited in number (in English there are forty-five vowels, consonants, and diphthongs) the economy is obvious.

Our word 'sun' has the same sound as 'son', and so in writing a distinction is made by the change of vowel. In some English words we have to distinguish the meaning by the context: e.g. 'fair'. Such words are homonyms. In ancient systems a clarifying device was used, namely the determinative, which could precede or follow the phonetic sign but was not pronounced. In Chinese the determinative, known as a radical, is embodied in the sign. There are 214 radicals used in teaching Chinese writing today. The Chinese language is basically monosyllabic and there are many words in it similar to others which have a different meaning. An example given by Professor W. Simon in *How to Study and Write Chinese Characters* is that the sound of the word for sheep is *yang* and is also the sound for ocean. So as to make the meaning of the character clear that ocean is intended and not sheep, a 'water radical' is incorporated in the phonetic symbol for *yang* (Plate 8).

The stages of development of writing did not run in a straight line of descent from pictures to alphabet, with each stage surplanting the earlier stage. There were mixed features in the transition, and, indeed, the Egyptians did not devise an alphabet though they reached a stage where letters (elements of an alphabet) were used. The story is complicated, conjectural, and confusing, and only clear in parts where knowledge has come by archaeological and lingual researches and the yield of remains. The outline and simple account in this book traces the handwriting of today, and particularly the italic hand, from beginnings in Sumer and Egypt, to the Phoenician invention of the alphabet and the writing of Greeks and Romans, and down to the Christian Era. The full story of what is now known is so extensive that it is not possible in this book to cover such systems as the Hittite hieroglyphs, the Indus Valley script, the Cretan hieroglyphs, Aztec writing, etc., though a glance aside at Chinese calligraphy seems appropriate and permissible because of its quality as an art.

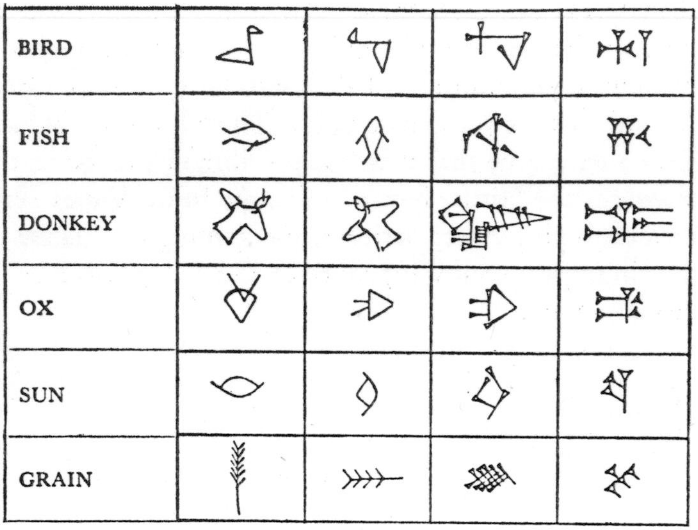

BIRD				
FISH				
DONKEY				
OX				
SUN				
GRAIN				

Fig. 1. Pictorial origin of some cuneiform signs. (From *A Study of Writing* by I. J. Gelb)

Sumerian Writing

Sumerian was the first language to be written and it is largely monosyllabic. The writing began as simple pictures and some can be traced to about 3100 B.C. How far back from this date picture-writing began is not yet clear for the earliest writing may have been scratched on wood and have decayed. Ideograms, phonograms, determinatives, and phonetic complements were used and indeed the Sumerians had established a full system of writing by about the middle of the third millennium B.C. Later in that millennium about a thousand symbols were in use in Uruk (the Biblical Erech, now named Warka), but this number may originally have been greater and in time reduced considerably. Each sign represented a word.

Sumer, the Land of Shiner in the Bible, may well be called the cradle of civilisation. It was but a small part of Southern Mesopotamia, lying at the head of the Persian Gulf, between the Rivers Euphrates and Tigris and within what is now Iraq. The highly original and gifted non-Semitic people of Sumer are appreciated today for their literature, myths, knowledge of mathematics, their curious ziggurat architecture, and much else. They may have come down from the Iranian mountains to form in time their city-states, one of which, Ur, is famous for its works of art. For 1500 years the Sumerians were influential in the Near East.

Much of the land of Sumer had been marsh and swamp and was irrigated. It was abundant in alluvial silt, deposited by floods and rivers on sedimentary rocks. The mud was excellent for cultivation, but also it was used as a writing material.

The surface of a formed lump of clay, shaped like a cushion and held in the hand, could be scratched to make signs. A better practice was adopted later which avoided the fragile edges thrown up by the scoring. This was done by pressing down the end of a triangular reed or other stylus so that it produced wedge-shaped strokes. This writing, changing from curved to linear forms, is called *cuneiform*, from the Latin word *cuneus*, meaning wedge. When baked, or dried in the hot sunshine, these tablets of clay were durable, and very many thousands have been discovered in good condition and can be read by scholars. Among the surviving Sumerian tablets are simple exercises in writing; but the earliest examples are lists of objects and relate to the economic activities of the priests of the Sumerian temples. Some of the characters were borrowed from the designs of seals.

An invention so convenient to commerce would impress neighbouring peoples when trading. The non-Semitic Elamites, and the Semitic Accadians (Babylonians and Assyrians), and later the Hittites and Persians, followed the Sumerians by writing in a cuneiform style. Fine examples of Mesopotamian inscriptions cut in stone exist which were carved by Babylonian and Assyrian Royal scribes.

Plates 1 and 2 are of early pictographic tablets of the Jemdet Nasr period of about 2800 B.C. Such early texts have not been fully deciphered but these are thought to be accounts of some kind. The tablet shown in Plate 3 is from 'Atshana (N. Syria) and is of the fifteenth century B.C. It concerns the settlement of a legal dispute between Abban and his sister Bittati over the division of property inherited from Ammurabi. The 'envelope' has the same text as the tablet and bears seal-impressions of the witnesses to the settlement. Figure 1 illustrates the transition of signs from pictograph to cuneiform.

Egyptian Writing

In ancient Egypt there were three scripts in use: hieroglyphic, hieratic, and demotic. The hieroglyphic style was used principally for sacred inscriptions on buildings and monuments. For a period of 3000 years down to Roman times the signs were carved in stone or painted with artistic discipline and little change in form. The characters include formalized pictures of men, animals, birds, household articles, tools, etc. and we can recognize them as such. They are the means of representing ideograms, phonograms, and determinatives, as word-signs or syllable signs. The characters did not include vowels. Some signs stood for consonants only and not for words or syllables (as seen in the cartouches of the Rosetta Stone) and were the elements of a possible alphabet that was not achieved.

Hieratic, deriving from the hieroglyphic, is explained by two circumstances. Papyrus was made from the pith of reeds and could be written on by brush and reed pen. Another economy was from the cursive principle. A more rapid style, the demotic, evolved from hieratic, and fluency caused a marked departure from the pictorial quality of hieroglyphs and even to the linking of signs. The hieratic system, used by priests, was in existence in the First Dynasty, but the demotic, the script of everyday affairs, has not been traced as existing earlier than the seventh century B.C.

Examples of the very beginnings of Egyptian writing have not yet been discovered but an early and important discovery was that of the Narmer ceremonial palette found in the temple of Hierakonpolis in Upper Egypt in 1898. This slate palette was carved on both sides about 2900 B.C., one side of which is shown in Figure 2. The king, wearing the crown of Upper Egypt and holding a mace, is striking an enemy. Here we have communication and recording by pictures but also, at top centre of the palette, a transitional semi-phonetic writing that could be read as 'Narmer'.

Hieratic writing changed from vertical columns to horizontal strips and was then directed from right to left.

Fig. 2
The Narmer Palette.
First Dynasty,
about 2900 B.C.
The top central
rectangle has signs
which could be
read as 'Narmer'.
Cairo Museum.
(From *A Study of
Writing* by
I. J. Gelb)

Chinese Calligraphy

The writing of China began with pictures which in time evolved into symbols that had lost their pictorial character, just as in Mesopotamian cuneiform and Egyptian demotic. The earliest known inscriptions had already passed the stage of pictographs and were made in the Shang-Yin Dynasty by astrologers for the purposes of divination (Plate 7). The inscriptions were scratched on bones and tortoise shells, and a Chinese scholar, Professor Ch'en Chih-Mai, has stated that 100,000 oracle bones have been excavated and on them over 2000 characters have been noted and 1,300 interpreted. The inscriptions on the oracle bones relate to many subjects: ancestor worship, war, expeditions, weather, birth, death, etc. Their date is about 1,100 B.C.

Bronze vessels of singular quality of design and workmanship, bearing valued inscriptions, were produced in the Chou Dynasty, which succeeded the Shang Dynasty in 1,027 B.C.

By the beginning of the Christian Era a highly developed script had been formed which has hardly changed. A person who could read Chinese would be able to read an inscription of the Former Han Dynasty of the second century A.D. There are several contemporary styles. Among Chinese calligraphers of the past are Emperors, Court and Government officials, for calligraphy has been highly esteemed.

The Chinese language is mainly monosyllabic and each character represents a whole word, whereas we use a number of signs (letters) to make words.

In China calligraphy has a great status as an art and some have regarded painting as but a branch of calligraphy. Mr. Hugh Gordon Porteus commented some years ago: 'When a Chinese calligrapher "copies" the work of an old master it is not a forged facsimile but an interpretation as personal within stylistic limits as a Samuel or Landowska performance of a Bach partita'. The copying of old writing is how calligraphers learn. The characters are abstract patterns, devised in the mind and written within the boundaries of the square. These units are placed and spaced in vertical columns starting from top right, the columns moving leftwards. The writing with its curves and angles is seen to have fluency, harmony, strength, balance, and a sophisticated and individual beauty. Chinese calligraphy is brushmanship and inkmanship and it has been said that the ink supports the brush and the brush supports the ink, which is a way of saying that they play their parts together. The brush has long hairs tapering to a sharp point. It is made so as to respond to sensitive pressures. Rabbit hair is popular for small writing and sheep hair for bold characters, but brushes are known to have been made of the hair of gorillas, tigers, wolves, and even of the whiskers of mice. The brush is held vertically but not necessarily so when painting pictures. Ink, dried into sticks or blocks, was also produced with care. The Emperor Chien Lung (A.D. 1736–93) would present ink-blocks to courtiers, moulded into exquisite but curious shapes quite unsuitable for the process of rubbing down the ink on a stone palette, but which would be valued as a gift of fine ink.

The calligraphic tradition in China is now under some strain, for it is reported that the Chinese are manufacturing fountain-pens on a mass-production scale. One wonders whether attempts at romanizing Chinese writing will ever be successful.

The Deciphering of Ancient Scripts

That difficulty should be experienced in deciphering ancient scripts is not surprising, for the language may be unknown, or the texts recovered may be insufficient, or the clues are few. Indeed, there are systems of writing which still cannot be elucidated or only partly deciphered. Among the many scholars who have sought to solve the enigmas there are three in particular who had outstanding successes: J. F. Champollion, H. C. Rawlinson, and M. Ventris.

In July 1799 a French officer of Engineers named Bouchard, serving in Napoleon's army, found a slab of black basalt in the fort of Saint Julien near Rosetta in the Nile Delta. The Rosetta Stone, broken in antiquity, has inscriptions in three texts and two languages: 14 lines of Egyptian hieroglyphs, 32 lines of demotic script, and 54 lines of Greek uncials (Figure 3). The obelisk was removed to Cairo where Napoleon had copies made for issue to European scholars. In 1802 the stone came to England under a Treaty of Capitulation, was deposited in the rooms of the Society of Antiquaries, and plaster casts were distributed. The stone was exhibited in the British Museum in the same year and is there still.

The texts are of a decree passed in the year 196 B.C. by the General Council of Egyptian Priests in honour of Ptolemy V, Epiphanes. The decree enumerates the benefits conferred by the King upon Egypt (gifts, remission or reduction of taxes, release of prisoners, rebuilding of sacred buildings, etc.) and records measures decided upon to do the King honour by statues, festivals, etc.

31

What can be faintly observed in Figure 3 are signs within ovals (cartouches). Thomas Young, a scientist of wide interests, had demonstrated that cartouches contained royal names and had deciphered the names of Cleopatra and Berenice inscribed in phonetic characters in another obelisk. However, the credit for the decipherment of hieroglyphs is accorded to a French scholar, Jean François Champollion (1790–1832), who identified the name of Ptolemy in the cartouches of the Rosetta Stone. By this key and his knowledge of Coptic, the last stage of the Egyptian language, he succeeded in translating the hieroglyphs of the memorial by 1821 and in making a dictionary.

As with hieroglyphs, the cuneiform scripts engaged the attention of a number of scholars before they could be read with ease. A German schoolmaster, George Friedrich Grotefend, had discovered a dozen sign meanings by 1815, but the true 'father' of cuneiform decipherment was Major (later Major General Sir) Henry Creswicke Rawlinson (1810–1895). While serving in Persia he studied three inscriptions on the Rock of Behistun, which record the achievements of Darius the Great (521–486 B.C.), and he published a translation in 1846. The texts of the inscriptions were in the languages of Old Persian, Elamite, and Accadian, and were written in different cuneiform systems. The story of his endeavours is one of determined persistence and also of athletic stamina and courage, for the inscriptions, cut in the rock face and associated with sculptures, were 300 feet above ground level. He copied the Persian text whilst in a perilous position on the topmost rung of a ladder. The ladder was standing on a narrow ledge of rock, not more than two feet wide, with a chasm below.

A great achievement, as recent as 1952, was that Michael Ventris (1922–56), an architect, in collaboration with Mr. John Chadwick and others, succeeded in deciphering clay tablets found in Mycenaean sites in Greece and Crete, inscribed with Linear B script, and in

1 & 2. Archaic tablets of the type found at Jemdet Nasr. About 2800 B.C. British Museum.

3. Tablet from 'Atshana with envelope. Fifteenth century B.C. The settlement of a legal dispute. The envelope bears seals of witnesses. British Museum.

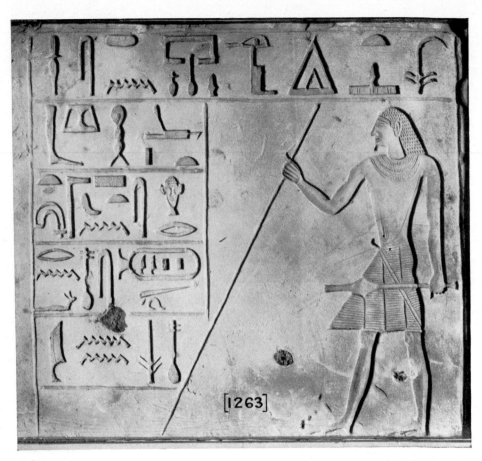

4. Limestone memorial with hieroglyphs from tomb of Senena, a 'Sole Companion and Chancellor' of Pepy II. About 2350 B.C. British Museum.

5. Hieratic script with an illustration from *The Book of the Dead of Ani*. Eighteenth Dynasty. British Museum.

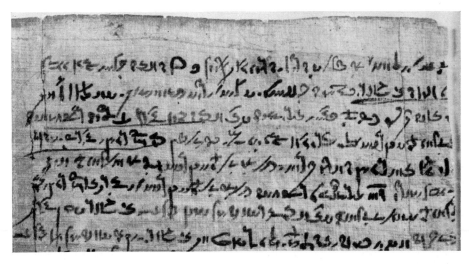

6. Demotic script. Proceedings of a Court of Justice. 23rd June 170 B.C. British Museum.

7. Chinese oracle bone. About 1100 B.C. British Museum.

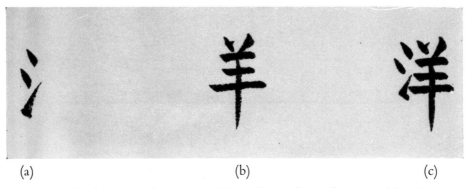

(a)   (b)   (c)

8. Water radical (a), sign for the word sheep (b), and sign for ocean (c) with water radical included. Written for this book by Mrs. Chi Chou Watts.

9. Phaistos Disc, from Crete. About 1700 B.C. Heraklion Museum.

10. Moabite Stone of Mesha, King of Moab. Mid ninth century B.C. The Louvre.

11. Etruscan alphabet written from right to left. Marsiliana abecedarium. About 700 B.C. Archaeological Museum, Florence.

12. Part of an Athenian *stoichedon* inscription. 408/7 B.C.

13. Inscription at the base of the Trajan Column, Rome. A.D. 114.

INTERQVASCVRAMCLYMENENAR
VOLCANIMARTISQ.DOLOSETDVLCI
ADQVECHAODENSOSDIVVMNVM
CARMINEQVOCAPTAEDVMFVSIM
DEVOLVVNTITERVMMATERNASIN
LVCTVSARISTAEIVITREISQ.SEDILI
OBSTIPVERESEDANTEALIASAREII
PROSPICIENSSVMMAFLAVVMCAT
ETPROCVLOGEMITVNONERVSTRA
CYRENESORORIPSETIBITVAMAX
TRISTISARISTAEVSPENEIGENITOR

14. Square capitals, with palimpsest. *Virgil*. Fourth century A.D. Library of St. Gall.

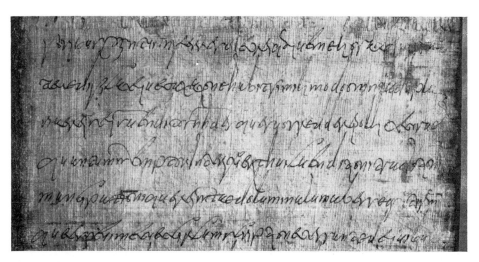

ERRABVNDABOVISVESTIGIAE
AVTHERBACAPTVMVIRIDIAN
PERDVCANTALIOSTABVLANT
TVMCANITHESPERIDVMMIR
TVMPHAETHONTIADASMVS
CORTICISATQVESOLOPROCER
TVMCANITERRANTEMPERM

15. Rustic capitals. *Virgil*. Fourth or fifth century A.D. Vatican Library.

16. Roman cursive writing, on papyrus. Deed of sale, Ravenna. A.D. 522. British Museum (Addl. MS. 5412).

PHARESAUTEMGE
NUITESROM
ESROMAUTEMGE
NUITARAM
ARAMAUTEMGENUIT
AMINADAB
AMINADABAUTEM
GENUITNAASSON
NAASSONAUTEMGE
NUITSALMON

ROBOAMAUTEMGE
NUITABIAM
ABIAAUTEMGENUITASA
ASAAUTEMGENUIT
IOSAPHAT
IOSAPHATAUTEM
GENUITIORAM
IORAMAUTEMGENUIT
OZIAM
OZIASAUTEMGENUIT

17. Uncials. Gospels. Eighth century A.D. British Museum (Addl. MS. 5463).

quodinterpretantur ētseptuaziīcai
quactantoetiamdiuinitursfaccominac
tauinecclesiisuetustacesinmetur;
Deluctuquodfecitioseph patris
XCII   exeodemlibroquaestionum de
E tfecitlu ctumpatrisuoseptemdies nesi
alicuiconamin scribtariscelebratu
quodapudlatinosnouendialappella
abhacconsuetudineprohibendisiqu
tuissuisunamenum seruantqurmas

18. Half-uncials. *Eugippio*. Sixth century A.D. Vatican Library (Vat. lat. 3375).

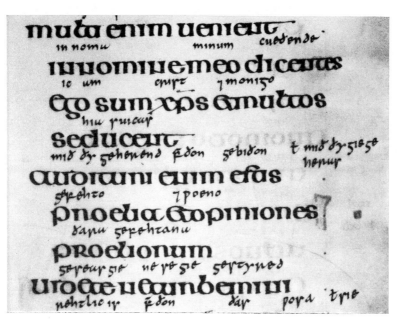

19. Insular half-uncials written by Eadfrith before A.D. 698. *The Lindisfarne Gospels.* The Anglo-Saxon translation written between the lines was by the priest Aldred in the tenth century. British Museum (Cotton MS. Nero D.IV).

20. Anglo-Saxon minuscules from Bede's *Historia Ecclesiastica Anglorum.* Eighth century A.D. British Museum (Cotton MS. Tib. C.II).

Duces caeci excolantes culicem camelum
autem glutuentes:
Uae uobis scribae et pharisaei hypocritae
qui tum mundatis quod deforis est calicis
et parabsidis· intus autem pleni sunt
rapina et inmunditia· pharisaeae cae
ce ·munda prius quod intus est calicis·

21. Caroline minuscules. Ninth century. British Museum.

Ben angeli dni dno. b celi dno·
Ben aquae omis quae sup celos
sunt dno. b omis uirtutes dni dno·
Ben sol & luna dno
benedicite stellae celi dno

22. From *The Ramsey Psalter*, written between A.D. 974 and 986. British Museum (Harley MS. 2904).

poreū ·uel ethera·uel tot
di habitū sup uolantis· S
ultra omīa que sunt· et c
usintime theologie per

23. From an Italian MS. of Homilies, etc. Twelfth century. British Museum (Harley MS. 7183).

doing so revealed that the language was an archaic form of Greek. Sir Arthur Evans had discovered at Knossos in Crete, at the beginning of the century, two cursive scripts which he differentiated as Linear A and Linear B. The language and the scripts were not known. Unlike Champollion, Ventris and his friends did not have the same text written in two languages for comparison. The problem of unravelling was most complicated, as we learn from John Chadwick's *The Decipherment of Linear B*.

The three decipherers referred to above showed at an early age a prophetic interest in the subjects of their successes. Champollion is reported as having said at the age of eleven that he was determined to decipher hieroglyphs some day. Rawlinson at the age of seventeen began to take an interest in Persian affairs. John Chadwick records that Ventris at the age of seven had bought a book on Egyptian hieroglyphs. When Ventris was fourteen he heard a lecture by Sir Arthur Evans on Crete and he began 'then and there to take up the challenge of the undeciphered Cretan writing'.

Among the scripts not yet deciphered is that of the fascinating and unique Phaistos Disc, found in 1908 by an Italian scholar, L. Permer, and dated to about 1700 B.C. This terracotta disc is about 6½in. in diameter and bears 31 groups of characters on one side (Plate 9) and 30 on the reverse side. The signs were made by pressing into clay punches of wood or metal, of which 45 different signs were used. (One may think of how a seal is pressed into sealing wax.) It is assumed that the writing is syllabic and that the spiral began from the rim.

The Etruscan alphabet is known, and is shown in Plate 11, but the language has not been deciphered.

Other ancient scripts have not yet yielded their secrets and these include the Cypro-Minoan scripts written in the Bronze Age in Cyprus, the Cretan Linear A, and the Indus Valley script of Northern India.

Fig. 3. The Rosetta Stone. An Egyptian decree in hieroglyphs, demotic characters, and Greek uncials. 196 B.C. British Museum

In 1947 shepherds found seven sheepskin scrolls in a cave near Qumran in the Judean Desert which came to be known as the Dead Sea Scrolls. Since then a large number of scrolls, documents and fragments, have been discovered in other caves, and these, because of their biblical and religious importance, have created great interest. The scripts, however, are known and are Hebrew and Aramaic, but the work of treatment, so that the scripts can be read, translated, and preserved, has been considerable. The Qumran documents are of the third century B.C. to A.D. 68.

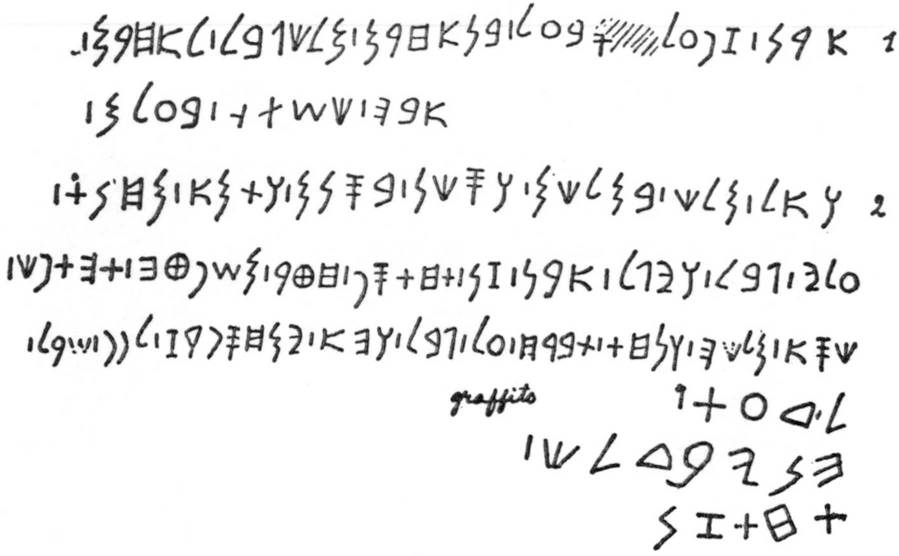

Fig. 4. Signs of the Early Phoenician alphabet from the Ahiram Sarcophogus and graffito. Byblos. Eleventh century B.C. Museum of Antiquities, Beirut. (From *A Study of Writing* by I. J. Gelb)

The Alphabet

An alphabet is a collection of letters, each one indicating one of the sounds used in speech. So, in a sense, writing speaks in the mind. If we write a long word like *incomprehensibleness* we use many letters to represent many sounds: not musical sounds making a melody, yet sounds that may be heard or imagined. The sounds follow one after the other like the letters. A language requires an adequate collection of various signs for its spoken sounds. English spelling-reformers say that we need 40 or more phonetic symbols in our alphabet, instead of the 26 we have. Sometimes a simple sound is indicated by two letters, such as *ch, sh, th, oo* (digraphs). We could spare the letters *Qq, Kk,* and *Xx*. Robert Bridges held that the diphthongal sound in the words *eye* and *right* has all manner of forms in our present spelling and he gave as examples *indictment, tie, eider, fly, dye, style, tile, sign, sigh, height, buy, ay, aisle, eying, eye*. Our *a* has to serve for four sounds (*day, all, and, father*) and *g* for two distinct consonants. The situation is complicated also by local or national ways of pronouncing vowels, and because sounds have varying musical pitch as syllables are accented. We do not drone on one note.

Was there an individual who invented the first alphabet? Is it possible that some genius, living far back in antiquity, whose name we shall never know, had the idea of making symbols represent simple spoken sounds and thus of words? The circumstances of the origin of the alphabet are still not known.

At Ugarit, now Râs Shamrah, on the Syrian coast, a large number of clay tablets have been found inscribed in a cuneiform writing style unlike any other known cuneiform writing. Among them a tablet discovered in 1949 is the oldest known example of a complete alphabet. This has 30 letters and was probably written in the fourteenth century B.C. Dr. David Diringer in his book *The Alphabet* suggests that this alphabet was invented by a person who knew an earlier North Semitic alphabet and was accustomed to the use of clay and stylus, or perhaps it was invented by the priests of Ugarit because they regarded cuneiform as correct for religious usage. A trustworthy starting-point for the history of the ancestral Phoenician alphabet was, in particular, the inscription on the sarcophagus of King Ahiram of Byblos, which may have been incised in the eleventh century B.C. and which has 22 signs (Fig. 4). However, Dr. Diringer suggests that a primitive Semitic alphabet probably originated in the period 1730–1580 B.C. and that in Byblos one or more attempts to introduce alphabetic writing were made in the Early Second Millennium B.C. There are many descendants of the Byblos alphabet including Arabic, Hebrew, and the Phoenician from which branch our alphabet descends.

In the Bible (2 Kings iii, 4–27) there is an account of how the Israelites put down a revolt by the Moabites. Mesha, King of Moab, gave a contrary description of the rebellion and this is preserved by the Moabite Stone in the Louvre, Paris. This inscription has 22 characters and is thought to have been made in the middle of the ninth century B.C. (Plate 10).

The view is now generally held that the Phoenician alphabet was influenced by Egyptian writing. In turn, the Phoenician alphabet influenced the writing of Greece and Rome. The Phoenicians were great sea-traders and did business about the Mediterranean and travelled as far west as Cornwall, where they obtained tin. Their alphabet may have been adopted in Greece about 1000 B.C. The Phoenician alphabet of 22 letters lacked vowels and it has been argued that for this reason it is not a complete alphabet. The Greeks added vowels to the consonants and thus brought the alphabet to a further stage of development. The first two signs of the Phoenician alphabet are named *aleph* and *beth*. The Greek names for letters derive from the Phoenician names and the Greeks called the first two letters of their alphabet *alpha* and *beta*, and from these names, which have no other meaning in Greek, we have the word *alphabet*. The Phoenician sign *aleph* is a glottal stop and not a consonant. As it was not required by the Greeks for its phonetic value it was made to serve as a vowel.

There were differences in alphabets as between Eastern and Western Greece. In 403 B.C., the Ionic form of the Eastern Greek alphabet was adopted in Athens and became the classical Greek alphabet of 24 letters. The Greek alphabet came to Italy among various places and there a Western Greek alphabet was used by the Etruscans.

The first civilization that flourished in Italy was that of the Etruscans, a mysterious people of unknown origin who were the predecessors of the Romans. The Etruscans may have received the Greek alphabet at the Greek colony, Cumae, near Naples. An interesting find at Marsiliana d'Alberga of an early abecedarium, dating from the seventh century B.C., is shown in Plate 11. This tablet was doubtless intended to be a pupil's model to copy, and shows the entire Etruscan alphabet of 26 letters written from right to left, which may be compared with the Moabite signs.

There was a time when early Greeks and Romans were alternating the direction of writing from line to line and reversing the letters as well as the direction so that E in one line became Ǝ in the next. This system of writing, which had ceased by the fifth century B.C., is called *boustrophedon*, a Greek word meaning 'ox turning'. The ox when ploughing is turned when it has crossed the field. This style, of course, doubled the shapes of many of the letters of their alphabets. Figure 21 taken from a Victorian booklet demonstrates the inconvenience of the style. This directional system would be just 'too much' to include in the Athenian *stoichedon* style of the fifth century B.C., where letters are seen in Plate 12 to be aligned vertically as well as horizontally from left to right.

Alphabets today may be different in appearance yet indicate the same set of sounds. Capitals are mostly different from the small letters (minuscules, or as the printers call them, lower case letters). There are other differences clearly to be seen in the following alphabets used in printing:

ABCDEFGHIJKLMNOPQRSTUVWXYZ
abcdefghijklmnopqrstuvwxyz

ABCDEFGHIJKLMNOPQRSTUVWXYZ
abcdefghijklmnopqrstuvwxyz

𝕬𝕭𝕮𝕯𝕰𝕱𝕲𝕳𝕴𝕵𝕶𝕷𝕸𝕹𝕺𝕻𝕼𝕽𝕾𝕿𝖀𝖁𝖂𝖃𝖄𝖅
abcdefghijklmnopqrstubwxyz

ABCDEFGHIJKLMNOPQRSTUVWXYZ
abcdefghijklmnopqrstuvwxyz

ABCDEFGHIJKLMNOPQRSTUVWXYZ
abcdefghijklmnopqrstuvwxyz

ABCDEFGHIJKLMNOPQRSTUVWXYZ
abcdefghijklmnopqrstuvwxyz

The Latin Scripts

An invention as valuable as that of the alphabet was bound to spread as did cuneiform writing, and so it passed on from the Greeks, via the Etruscans, to the Romans. Some of the letters used by the Etruscans were discarded and at the time of the Roman Republic the alphabet had 21 letters, A to X, but later the Romans added Y and Z. We have inherited this alphabet of 23 letters but it was extended to 26 to include J, U, and W. These three additions were made in the Middle Ages and grew from the letters I and V.

The oldest known Roman inscription was probably made in the 7th century B.C. and is on the Praeneste gold brooch, where the letters run from right to left. The inscription is, when transcribed: MANIOS: MED: FHEFHAKED: NVMASIOI, which translated is: 'Manius made me for Numerius'. Certain letters of this inscription indicate that the Latin alphabet came from Etruscan script (Figure 5).

Because inscriptions appeal to the eye, it follows that in the

Fig. 5. The Praeneste gold brooch, made by Manius for Numerius. Seventh century B.C. Museo Pigorini, Rome

course of hundreds of years of use both the Greek and the Roman alphabet developed in design and grace. Eventually the Roman letters reached a standard of form that still gains the highest admiration of letterers, calligraphers, and printers. The favourite example of classic Roman capitals, cut in A.D. 114 with exquisite skill and craftsmanship in a hard stone, is seen in the inscription near the base of the Trajan Column in Rome (Plate 13). There is hardly a good contemporary book on lettering which does not have an illustration of this superb inscription. The form of every letter is familiar to us, for not only has the hardness of stone preserved the shapes of letters from decay but the invention of printing and the use of printing-types based upon Roman capitals have kept them from obsolescence.

The forms of the Roman capitals reflect the use of the tool that cut them, the chisel, but the incidence of thicks, thins, and the gradations of curved strokes relate to those a broad brush or pen would make.

A palaeographer is a historian of ancient scripts. Palaeographers refer to majuscules and minuscules. Capitals are majuscules and seem bounded by two imaginary horizontal lines. Minuscules developed from majuscules but are written as if between four lines because of their extended parts, which ascend or descend: i.e. the ascenders and descenders. The oldest Latin majuscule writing as found in early manuscripts is in rustic capitals and square capitals (Plates 14 and 15). The tendency to write with speed and consequently to simplify when writing informally, produced cursive script. Such cursive writing has been found in papyrus documents, scratched on stucco walls, and on wax tablets, etc. (Plate 16).

Very little remains that was written in square capitals, which are near in shapes to the carved capitals, and this script may have been reserved for the finest manuscripts. Rustic capitals are narrower letters written more freely and having thin down strokes and heavy bases. This script was the usual book-hand of the Roman Empire, and dates from the first to the sixth centuries A.D.

Two other literary hands of the Roman Empire are uncials and half-uncials (Plates 17 and 18). A famous palaeographer, the late B. L. Ullman, in *Ancient Writing and its Influence*, has likened the square capitals to a father and Roman cursive to a mother. Rustic takes after a stiff and formal father, Square Capital, rather than a slatternly mother, Cursive, but the 'second child which grew up and prospered was Uncial'. Another descendant was the half-uncial and it survived and became famous.

At its best the uncial script is splendid, as can be seen in Plate 17: rounded, clear, strong, and with a marked pen-character. Manuscripts written in uncials between the fourth and eighth centuries A.D., with texts both sacred and profane, are surprisingly numerous: five hundred manuscripts including fragments exist. The uncial letters ADEHMU have distinctive curved shapes.

The half-uncial hand, the fifth of the Latin scripts, has ascenders and descenders, but there are contrary views as to whether it is to be called a majuscule or minuscule hand. The earliest known half-uncial script was written not later than A.D. 510. It may have sprung up in North Africa in the fourth century. After it had passed to Ireland and England it is appreciated for the superb script of the *Lindisfarne Gospels* (Plate 19) and of the later Irish *Book of Kells*. In contrast to the round letters of the uncials are the narrowed Anglo-Saxon cursive letters represented in Plate 20. There were other national hands stemming from the Latin scripts written in Italy, Spain, Germany, and France. Of these, the Carolingian minuscules have had enormous influence.

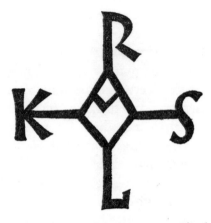

Fig. 6a. Monogram of the Emperor Charlemagne as used on documents. From *A Book of Signs* by Rudolf Koch

The Carolingian and Mediaeval Scripts

In France by the end of the eighth century A.D. there had arisen a script called Carolingian or Caroline, which stands out in our heritage along with Roman capitals because of the ultimate effect of this style on alphabets of today. The earliest version is in the Bible written for Abbot Maurdramnus of Corbie who died in 778. The Caroline hand, seen in a ninth-century version in Plate 21, sprang largely from half-uncial but had at first some cursive characteristics. However, in time the script became quite formal. The name of the style relates to the Emperor Charlemagne, for it was in use under his patronage. Christian and classical manuscripts were copied at the Monastery of St. Martin at Tours, where Alcuin of York was Abbot from A.D. 796 to 804. Noble versions of the Carolingian script were used in Southern England in the tenth century (Plate 22). Plate 23 shows a twelfth-century version written in Northern Italy.

The scripts of the Middle Ages became compressed and angular. There are many versions. Whilst Gothic writing was sometimes ornamental, it is not so clear as the Caroline scripts and at worst was hard to read and lifeless. (The name 'Gothic' was used by Renaissance scholars in contempt as meaning barbarous.) Plate 24 shows a Gothic script and an illuminated letter with an heraldic device, which links the teaching of the alphabet with the Lord's Prayer. This prayer-book, written about A.D. 1386, is in the Bodleian Library, Oxford. Gothic lettering still has some use: we may find it in church notices and newspaper headings. A fortunate circumstance is that the English secretary hand, a mediaeval cursive used for ordinary purposes in the time of Elizabeth I, died out in the seventeenth century. It is the hand which Shakespeare wrote. A model of alphabets of the secretary hand by Jean de Beauchesne is illustrated in Figure 6. Other mediaeval scripts were used in England for particular purposes of administration, and were different according to the several offices. These were Court hands (cf. page 9 5).

Fig. 6b. English secretary hand. From *A Booke Containing Divers Sortes of Hands* by Jean de Beauchesne. 1570

The Scripts of the Italian Renaissance

The Italian Renaissance began in the fourteenth century and this great movement in the long history of civilization brought about in the fifteenth century important changes in handwriting styles. A fresh interest was taken in classical Latin literature and accordingly searches were made for manuscripts of the classic authors which had been perhaps neglected and forgotten; when found, these were copied by the humanists. Petrarch and Coluccio Salutati reformed their script in a style known as *fere humanistica* (almost humanistic), for they were critical of the Gothic writing. Later, Poggio Bracciolini (1380–1459) wrote a book-hand in 1402 which derived from a late Carolingian style found in Italian manuscripts of the eleventh or twelfth centuries (cf. Plate 23). In adopting this clear style, known to palaeographers as 'humanistic', Poggio is given credit for inventing the roman letter, which ultimately was produced as the lower case printing type (Plate 25). Poggio's script has oblique shading in the curves of the letters and the thickest strokes are not the vertical ones, as they are in the script illustrated in Plate 28 and in many later roman scripts. The Renaissance scholars and penmen called the roman style *lettera antiqua* in the belief that the Caroline writing they had come to admire was of classical antiquity.

The earliest example of italic writing (humanistic cursive) is that of a Florentine scholar, Niccolò Niccoli, and he is regarded as the inventor. He used diagonal joins such as are found in the sort of mediaeval cursive hand he would have been taught in his youth and he incorporated them in the humanistic hand (Plate 26). This was an expression of the cursive principle. Whether Niccoli's practice was recognized and led on to the italic hand of the sixteenth century is not established. There is evidence that when the roman script was written quickly the proportions and shapes of the letters began to change through the avoidance of pen-lifts and the use of upstrokes and joins and thus a new style of writing was developed.

Among scribes engaged in the second half of the fifteenth century in making books which were written in an early style of italic handwriting were Pietro Cennini, Antonio Tophio, and Bartholomeo San Vito. Plate 29 shows Tophio's italic hand: like other scribes he also wrote fine versions of roman script.

Many years passed after Niccoli's death in 1437 before the italic hand, used both in making manuscript books and in writing documents, reached the point of excellence. Two other fine examples of the italic script are shown in Plates 30 and 31. The first was by an unknown scribe of the Vatican Chancery and was written about 1490. The second is from a Papal brief dated 27 August 1519 addressed to Cardinal Wolsey and which has reference to the Bishop of Winchester. The script of this brief is attributed to Ludovico degli Arrighi (sometimes known as Vicentino) and is in the *cancellaresca* (chancery) hand which he taught by the first printed book to give instruction in the writing of this script: *La Operina*, published in Rome in 1522 (Figure 7). This book has been much admired and indeed has been reproduced five times in different facsimiles during this century. A second manual by this revered scribe, *Il Modo*, gave examples of various scripts.

Books began to be printed by movable types in the fifteenth century. The invention of printing is credited to Johann Gutenberg of Mainz at about the year 1450 (though claims have been made that Laurens Coster of Haarlem was the inventor). In one of his publications Gutenberg stated that printing had been accomplished without the help of reed, stylus, or pen. However, the types he and other

24. Gothic alphabet and script from a prayer-book. About 1386. Bodleian Library (MS. Rawl. liturg. e 40, 15829). From *Florilegium Alphabeticum* by B. L. Wolpe in *Calligraphy and Palaeography*.

25. Humanistic (roman) script of Poggio Bracciolini. *Cicero*. 1425. Bibl. Laur., Florence (Plut. 50. 31). From *Renaissance Handwriting*.

26. Italic script of Niccolò Niccoli. *Lucretius*. ?1423. Bibl. Laur., Florence (Laur. 35, 30).

In expeditionibus tantum ad sui tutelam
alterius lesionem commodum est hostium
condicionem nosse ac statum . ideoq; nulla
utilior impensa q̃ in exploratore fideli ac
cauto . aut in transfuga simulato . Incongru
um uidetur imperatoris militem qui ueste
et annona publica pascitur . utilitatibus ua
care priuatis . Omnium cohortium equitũ

27. Roman script of Giacomo Curlo. *Vegetius*. Before 1458. Bodleian Library
(Canon. lat. 274).

oratio &operatio ad te semper
incipiat: &per te cepta finiat͞.
Mnipotens Oratio·
sempiterne deus qui
uiuorum dominaris
simul &mortuorum: omniuq;
misereris: quos tuos fide & o
pere futuros esse prenoscis: te

28. Roman script of Alexander Antonii Simonis.
Book of Hours. 1477. British Museum (Yates
Thompson 6).

chel tempo spensi, et tennonsi legiadri
Chempallidir fel tempo et morte amara
L oblunon laspecti oscuri et atri
Pui chemai bei tornando lascieranno
A morte mpetuosa igiorni ladri
N elleta pui fiorita et uerde haranno
Con mortal belleza eterna fama
Ma inanzi a tutte charisar seuanno
E t quella chepiangendol mondo chiama
Con lamia lingua et collastanca penna
Ma ilciel pur di uederla interra brama
A ruia un fiume chenasce ingebenna
Amor midie per lei si lunga guerra
Che lamemoria anchor ilcor accenna
F elice sasso chelbel uiso serra
Che poi chaura ripreso ilsuo beluelo
S efu beato chi lauide interra
O rchefia dunque a riuederla incielo.

: ΤΕΛΩΣ :

I ncipiunt euisdem quædam dicta reperta
inquodam Virgilio in Papiensi bibliotheca
ipsius manu propria scripta ut fertur

29. Italic hand of Antonio Tophio. Petrarch: *Poems*. Montpellier
Medical Library.

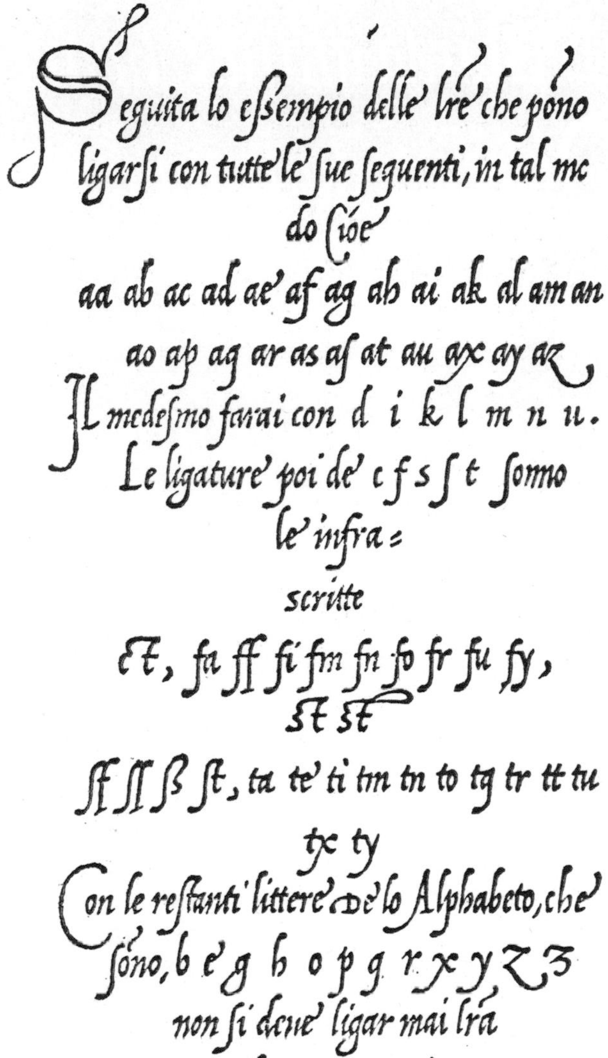

Seguita lo essempio delle lre che pono
ligarsi con tutte le sue seguenti, in tal me
do cioe

aa ab ac ad ae af ag ah ai ak al am an
ao ap aq ar as af at au ax ay az
Il medesmo farai con d i k l m n u.
Le ligature poi de c f s f t somno
le infra=
scritte

ct, fa ff fi fm fn fo fr fu fy,
st st

ff ff ß ft, ta te ti tm tn to tg tr tt tu
te ty
Con le restanti littere De lo Alphabeto, che
sono, b e g h o p g r x y z z
non si deue ligar mai lra
alcuna seguente

Fig. 7. From *La Operina* by Ludovico degli Arrighi.
1522. Rome

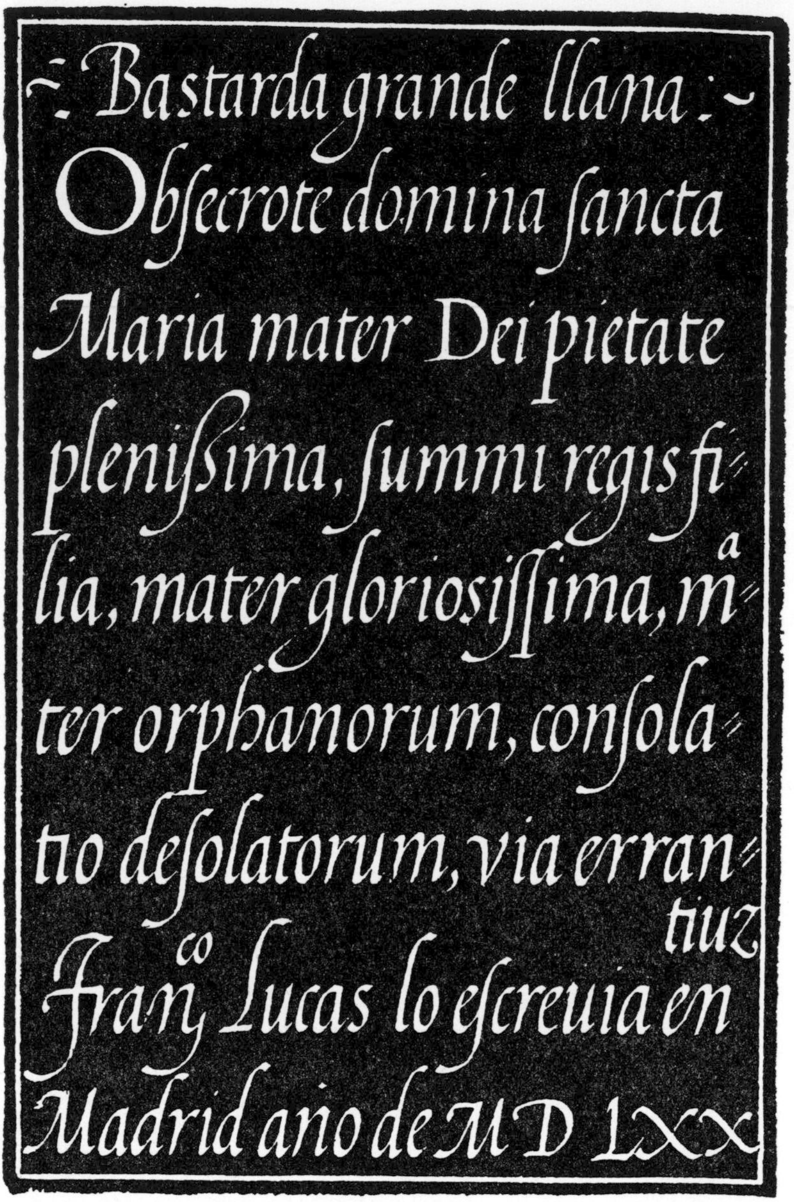

~: Bastarda grande llana :~

Obsecrote domina sancta
Maria mater Dei pietate
plenissima, summi regis fi-
lia, mater gloriosissima, m^{a}-
ter orphanorum, consola-
tio desolatorum, via erran-
tiuz
Fran^{co} Lucas lo escreuia en
Madrid año de M D LXX

Fig. 8. From *Arte de escriver* by Francisco Lucas. Published in 1577.
Madrid

early printers used were imitations of Gothic and humanistic scripts. Moreover, not only the letter-forms but the general design of the splendid manuscript books of the time were models that were familiar and respected. The clarity of the printing of this very book owes a debt to Renaissance scribes.

The invention of printing, the mass mechanical production of 'writing', did not destroy what it imitated but led to more extensive use of the pen by the spread of learning.

Arrighi, Ferdinando Ruano, and other scribes produced manuscript books of distinction in the first half of the sixteenth century, although by then a large number of books had been printed and scribes were much less needed.

Aldus Manutius, the Venetian printer, produced a series of small books printed in italic, the first of which, a *Virgil*, appeared in 1501. The type was based upon an italic hand which may possibly have been that of Pomponio Leto, a leading scholar and the founder of the Roman Academy. Later italic types, designed by Arrighi, have been praised by the historians of printing.

The italic hand was adopted in countries distant from Italy and as far apart as Poland and England. In England it was first used by those who were at the Royal Court or had travelled in Italy or were at the Universities. When Henry VIII came to the throne the italic hand was already in use in the Court by Italian secretaries. His children, Edward VI and Elizabeth I, were taught to write in this style by Roger Ascham and Plate 32 gives an example of Elizabeth's elegant script, in a letter, unhappily partly burnt, to Thomas Seymour. The Duke of Richmond wrote an impressive version at the age of eight under the guidance of Richard Croke. At Cambridge, owing to the influence of Sir John Cheke and Roger Ascham, many of the scholars wrote their important letters in a careful italic hand. The most notable of these as a penman was Bartholomew Dodington, a Professor of Greek and an accountant. Plate 33 is of a letter from the young Earl of Essex to Lord Burghley written at the age of nine just after the death of his father.

The first writing book to be printed in England was by Jean de Beauchesne, a Huguenot who settled in London. His book of examples of scripts *A Booke Containing Divers Sortes of Hands* was published in 1570 and shows among the various scripts the 'Italique hande' (Plate 34) and the English secretary hand commonly used at the time (Figure 6). A page of a Spanish writing-book by Francisco Lucas is reproduced in Figure 8. His book is often studied by calligraphers today.

Fig. 9. Portrait of Charles I by Joseph Goddard.
?1644. British Museum (Sloane 994)

READING and WRITING.

By the Arts of Reading and Writing, we can Sit at Home and acquaint our selves with what is done in all the distant Parts of the World, & find what our Fathers did long ago in the first Ages of Mankind.

Fig. 10. From *The Universal Penman* by George Bickham. 1733–41

Copperplate Writing

Copperplate is a word sometimes used to refer to any careful, neat and disciplined handwriting, but this definition is too wide. The models in the earliest printed copy-books were reproduced by engraved wood blocks (see Figure 7), but in the second half of the sixteenth century some manuals showed exemplars printed from engraved metal plates. This later method of reproduction, coupled with changing taste, modified the style of the italic hand through the tools and methods involved in engraving metal plates. Soon the pen was expected to make letters which were imitations of engraving. Some engravers' strokes were but the merest scratches and others dug well into the plate. The deeper the cut the wider the stroke. A sharply pointed pen was necessary to imitate the engraved letters. The width and variations of the penstrokes depended upon how heavy or how light was the pressure put upon the pen's point. Therefore the pupil had to learn not only to make the shapes but also to control the pressure of pen-point on paper. If the father of copperplate is the italic hand, the copperplate child left home to be in servitude to the engraver's needle. The example by John Davies of Hereford in Plate 35 shows the child leaving home.

Another feature of copperplate hands are the loops to ascenders, which began to appear in writing models at the beginning of the seventeenth century. Ultimately the aim was to write words with one continued line: i.e. without pen-lifts. Indeed copy-books can be named where the line did not end with the word but linked with the succeeding word. During the seventeenth century, writing-books often showed models decorated by drawings of men, animals, birds, fish, etc. made by flourishing of pen-stokes, known as 'command of hand'. Figure 9 is of a head of Charles I made by Joseph Goddard in 1644 when aged 15 and a pupil at the Writing School of Christ's Hospital. These flourishes by Goddard were 'invented, ordered and composed by Jonathan Pickes, Writing Master', who taught Goddard twelve different scripts.

As English trade grew, more people needed to write, and many copy-books were produced. The most notable production in the eighteenth century is George Bickham's *The Universal Penman*, which was issued in parts from 1733 to 1741 and has 212 large pages printed from metal plates, presenting the work of twenty-five penmen (Figure 10).

Early in the nineteenth century, two rival writing-masters were James Henry Lewis of Ebley, near Stroud, and Joseph Carstairs. Both claimed Royalty as patrons, and Carstairs persuaded the Duke of Kent in 1816 to attend a meeting at which the Duke said he had directed several poor boys, who had made little progress in writing, to be under the superintendence of Carstairs. Of their rapid and extraordinary progress he could speak in the most confident manner. Carstairs had a considerable success in the U.S.A. with his system.

Figure 11 shows examples of nineteenth-century models by other writing-masters given by John Jackson as a critical illustration of their 'disgraceful diversity of slant' in his book *The Theory and Practice of Handwriting*, first published in 1892 and which advocated a vertical hand. A much more severe criticism was made by Robert Bridges, the poet, who regarded Victorian school copy-books as soulless models and held that the ultimate degradation was won in lawyers' offices where clerks 'scrupulously perfected the very most ugly thing that a conscientious civilisation has ever perpetrated'.

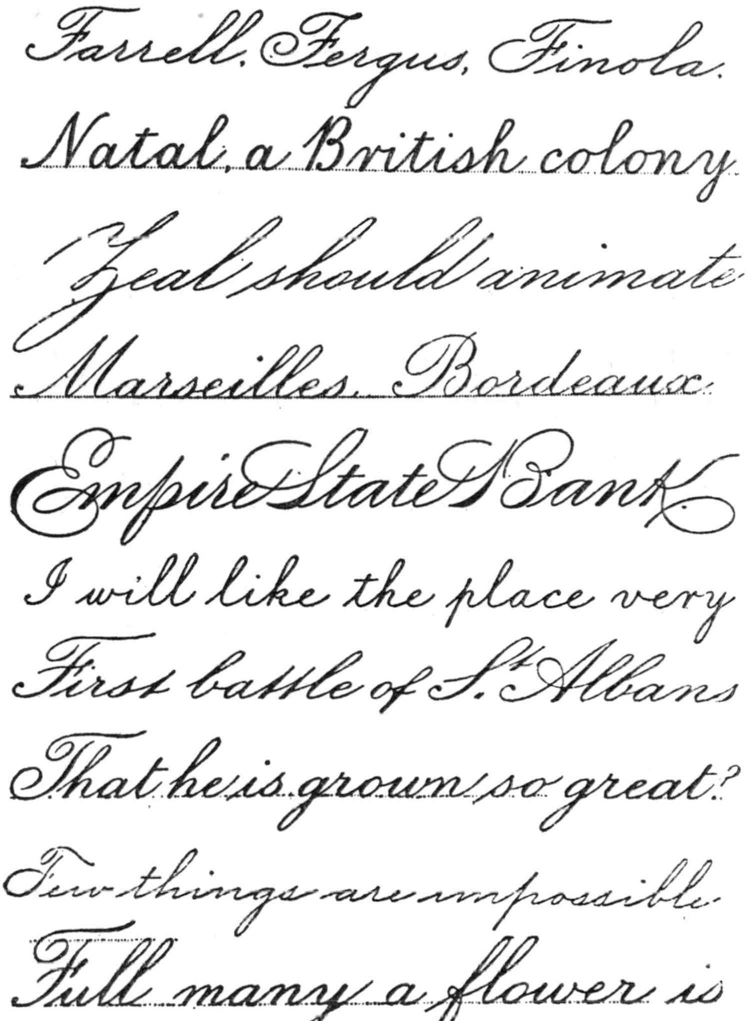

Farrell. Fergus, Finola.

Natal, a British colony.

Zeal should animate.

Marseilles. Bordeaux.

Empire State Bank.

I will like the place very

First battle of S.t Albans

That he is grown so great?

Few things are impossible.

Full many a flower is

Fig. 11. Examples of copperplate hands from *The Theory and Practice of Handwriting* by J. Jackson. 1898

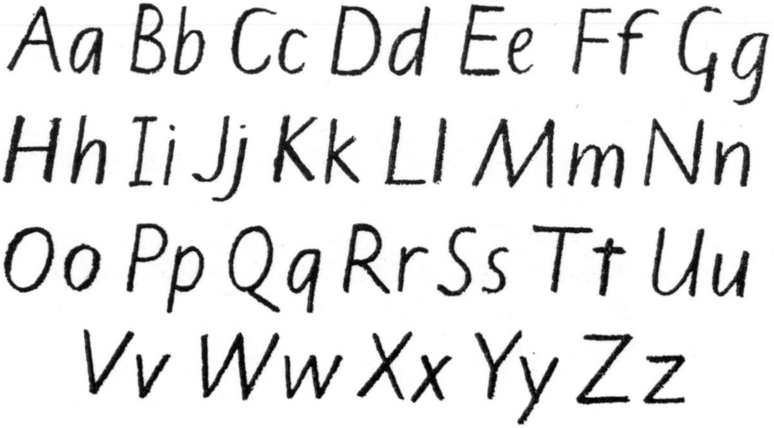

Aa Bb Cc Dd Ee Ff Gg
Hh Ii Jj Kk Ll Mm Nn
Oo Pp Qq Rr Ss Tt Uu
Vv Ww Xx Yy Zz

Fig. 12. Italic alphabets for teaching infants. From *Beacon Writing Book No. Two*

Print-script

In 1913 Edward Johnston was asked to address a conference of London teachers on the teaching of handwriting. In putting forward an ideal scheme (it proved too difficult for teachers to adopt) he showed among other alphabets the skeleton or essential shapes of the Roman alphabets. It was seen that a simplification of letter-forms might be adopted for teaching beginners to write and this would also help children to learn to read. By 1916 experiments had begun in London schools. The style, now known as print-script, soon spread widely in this and other countries. Miss Marjorie Wise introduced a form of it into the United States of America, where it is known as manuscript writing.

Although useful for teaching infants, print-script has a serious lack as a handwriting style, for it does not develop naturally into a running hand. Accordingly, some other style is generally taught when the child uses a pen. Print-script is plainly uueconomical since it has to be abandoned and a poor foundation for the acquisition of a fundamental skill.

Attempts have been made to add joins to print-script but with little success. A system was devised by the late Marion Richardson which was to introduce the child to a style having some relationship to both print-script and italic by the use of writing patterns.

An experiment brought into English schools by Sir James Pitman as a means of teaching the infant to read is the 'initial teaching alphabet' (i.t.a.). This alphabet has forty characters to represent as many sounds. It is claimed that when the child has learned to read a transition can be made to the traditional alphabet. The i.t.a.

phonetic symbols have been incorporated in print-script, but they could be written in italic style.

In the view of the author, what would be appropriate for beginners would be a very simple italic print-script, following prewriting exercises. Such a style could lead on from infancy to maturity (Figure 12).

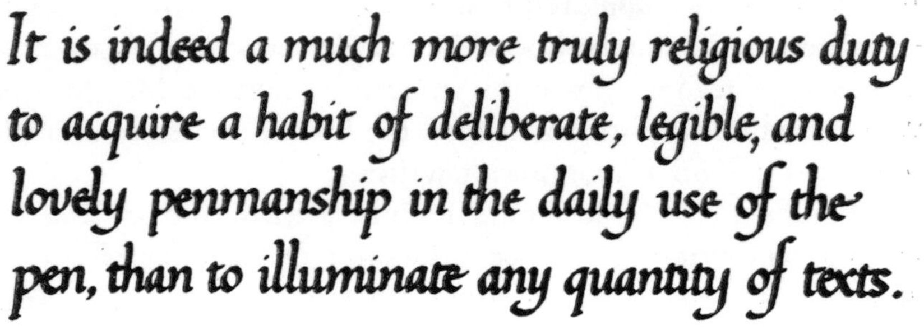

It is indeed a much more truly religious duty to acquire a habit of deliberate, legible, and lovely penmanship in the daily use of the pen, than to illuminate any quantity of texts.

Fig. 13. Italic hand of Graily Hewitt. 1916

The Italic Hand of Today

The revival of the italic hand of the Italian Renaissance began when William Morris, the Victorian poet and craftsman, was engaged in making a number of what he called 'painted books', which in fact were illuminated manuscripts. This was during the period 1870 to 1875. Morris bought a volume made up of four Italian sixteenth-century writing-books, namely Ugo da Carpi's version of Arrighi's *La Operina*, Arrighi's *Il Modo*, G. A. Tagliente's *Opera che insegna a scrivere*, and Sigismundo Fanti's *Thesauro*. He is known to have studied Arrighi's model but to have made his own version of the italic hand, and to have used it in transcribing a *Horace*, now in the Bodleian Library, and a copy of his translation of a saga *King Hafbur & King Siward* in the Fitzwilliam Museum, Cambridge. A fragment of the *Arabian Nights*, written by Morris, with an incomplete initial, is shown in Plate 37. In 1898 Mrs. M. M. Bridges, the wife of another famous poet, Robert Bridges, published a book called *A New Handwriting for Teachers* and this introduced the italic hand into a number of English schools (Plate 38). In 1906 Edward Johnston published his masterly book *Writing & Illuminating, & Lettering* and he gave illustrations of an Italian 'semi-formal' hand which could be called italic. Copy-books were produced by Graily Hewitt in 1916 but he taught that every letter should be made separately. This restriction was against cursive fluency (Figure 13). These models were followed in 1932 by those in the author's own book *A Handwriting Manual* and his copy-cards. Now there are instructions in writing the italic hand published in the U.S.A., Holland, Denmark, and S. India, as well as others in Great Britain.

Not only is the hand taught in many schools, but there is a Society for Italic Handwriting with membership in numerous countries.

The person learning the italic hand needs an italic nib to gain the best result, and stationers stock several makes of fountain-pens at small cost which take italic nibs. The learner must hold the pen so that the thinnest stroke the pen makes runs up to the right at an angle of 45 degrees (but not less) to the writing line. An easy test as to whether the pen is correctly held is to cross a vertical stroke with a horizontal stroke so that both strokes are equally thick: ✚
If the vertical stroke is thinner, turn the pen slightly to the body. If the horizontal stroke is thinner, turn the pen slightly from the body.

The italic letters are not so wide as roman or print-script letters and their proportions are not related to the square or circle. The letter 'o' is elliptical. Downstrokes should have only a slight slope forward. (See Figure 14.)

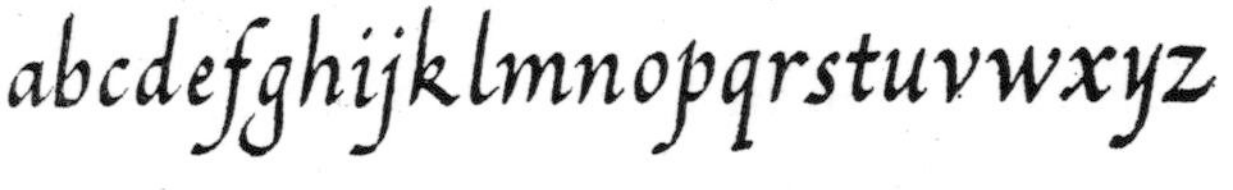

abcdefghijklmnopqrstuvwxyz

Fig. 14. Italic alphabet from *Beacon Writing Book No. Five*

The alphabet is best learnt by grouping letters according to the principal movements which shape them. The groups are *ilt, adgqu, ceo, mnr, bhk, vwy, fs, jp, xz*. The simple letters of the first group end

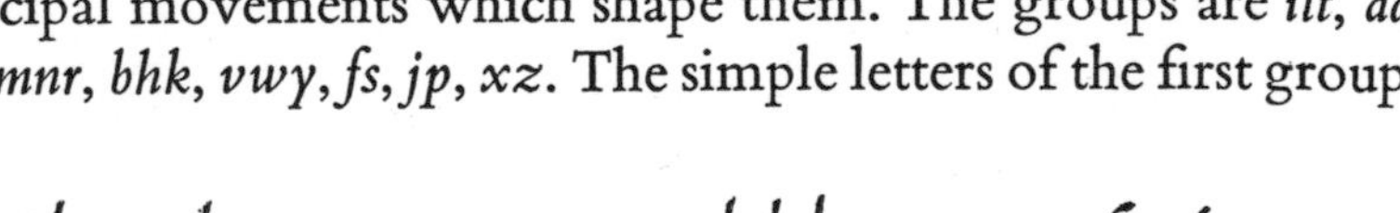

ilt adgqu ceo nmr bhk vwy fs jp xz

with a narrow bend (not a point) and the stroke upwards stops as soon as it becomes a hairline. An important feature of the second and third groups *adgquceo* is the counter-clockwise movement at the bases of the letters. Here again, there are narrow bends and not sharp pointed angles. The letters *mnrbhk* have a clockwise movement springing from the base of the first downstroke. The reader may be reminded of a rocket or a jet of water going up and then turning to the right in a curve before dropping. Again the turning movement does not make an angle or a part of a circle but a narrow curving bend. The letter *r* could easily be made too like a *v* when written quickly, so the pen must return well up the downstroke before branching away. The letters *vwy* do have an angular base at the learning stage. The letters *f* and *s* both begin and end the downstroke by moving to the left. The *f*, like the *t*, should be crossed at the height of the letter *o* and not higher. The *p* could be made without a pen-lift by omitting the turn of the descender to the left and by returning up the long downstroke. The letter *x* is made of two strokes, and the *z* zigzags.

Joins are required for quick writing. The two principal joining strokes are the diagonal and horizontal. If letters *n* are written it is plain that an extension of the last stroke will join the letter to the next: *nnnm*. The join will be oblique. Such joins would naturally follow on from *acdehiklmntu*. The drills suggested on page 98 would be good practice. If the word to be written is (say) *town*, three horizontal joins are used, the first being an extension of the cross-stroke of the *t*: *town*. (The cross-stroke of an *f* will similarly make a join.) Some letters, because of their shape, do not join up easily or suitably, consequently letters are joined or not joined according to what is convenient at the moment of writing. Wherever linking strokes can be made it is sensible to use them, for they are necessary for speedy writing. The letter *e* may be made with two strokes, the first being nearly straight and the second a small bow which can run on: *ceen*. The virtue of this method is that it helps to avoid blobbing and to space letters, and is not altogether uneconomical.

63

ABCDEFGHIJKLMNOPQRS TUVWXYZ

Fig. 15. Italic capitals from *Beacon Writing Book No. Five*

The simple capitals in Figure 15 are without serifs and have the same slant as the small letters.

A less simple but freer alphabet of capitals is shown in Figure 16. The flourishes will be seen to be restrained and not too decorative, and the letters are not obtrusive.

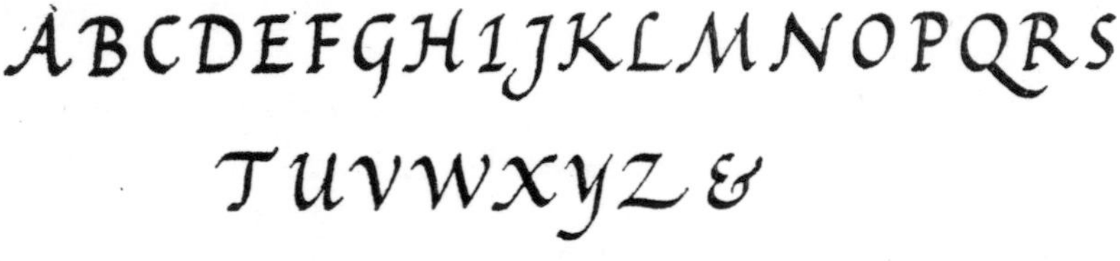

ABCDEFGHIJKLMNOPQRS TUVWXYZ &

Fig. 16. Flourished capitals from *Beacon Writing Book No. Five*

Figure 17 shows punctuation marks, numerals, etc. At the end of the line of stops there is a very simple ampersand: a sign for the word *and*. The word ampersand is said to be a corruption of the

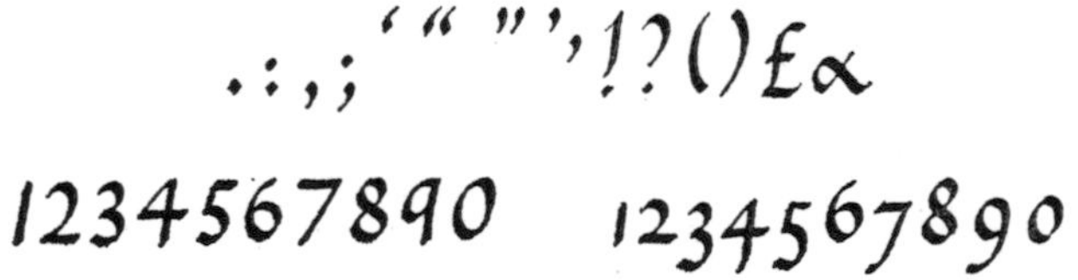

. : , ; ' " " ' ! ? ( ) £ &

1234567890   1234567890

Fig. 17. Punctuation marks and numerals from *Beacon Writing Book No. Five*

64

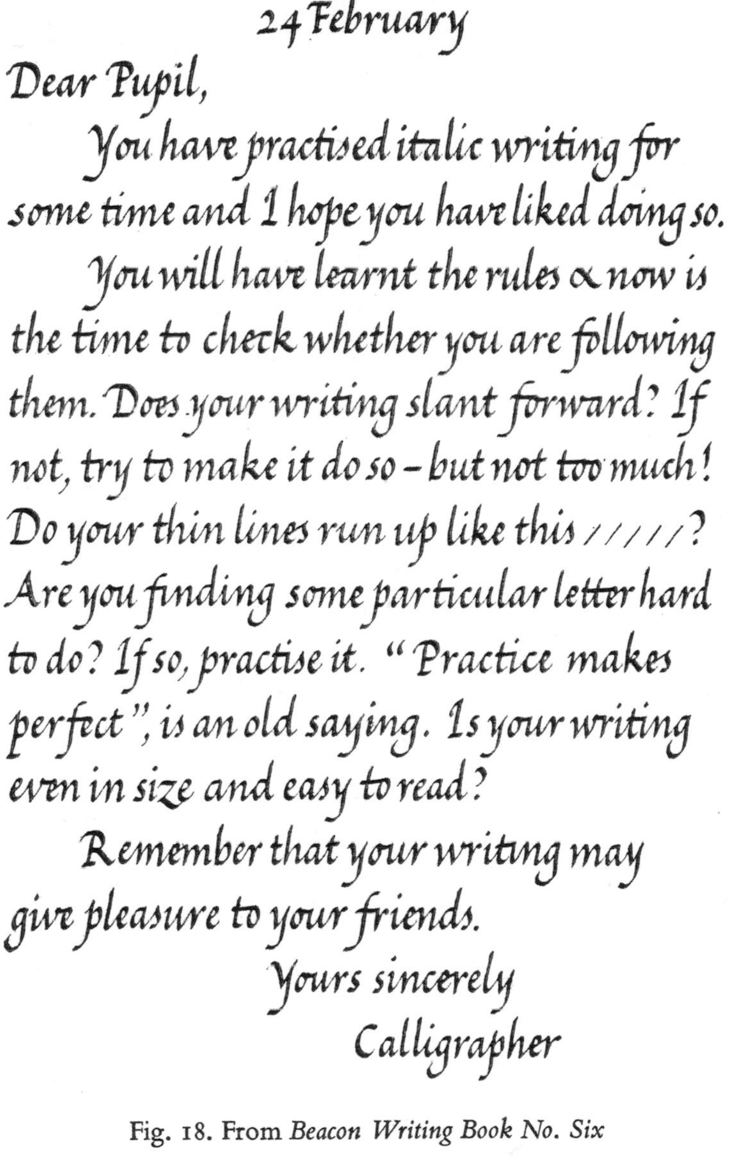

18 Bedford Row, London, W.C.1

24 February

Dear Pupil,

You have practised italic writing for some time and I hope you have liked doing so.

You will have learnt the rules & now is the time to check whether you are following them. Does your writing slant forward? If not, try to make it do so – but not too much! Do your thin lines run up like this /////? Are you finding some particular letter hard to do? If so, practise it. "Practice makes perfect", is an old saying. Is your writing even in size and easy to read?

Remember that your writing may give pleasure to your friends.

Yours sincerely

Calligrapher

Fig. 18. From *Beacon Writing Book No. Six*

phrase 'and *per se* and', which might be recited after the alphabet, and meaning that the sign 'and' was not used for connecting parts of a sentence but for itself alone. The numerals of the first set are written as between two imaginary lines and the second set as between four lines. The first set, the practical one, would be generally used, whilst the second set, which is related to the numerals to be seen in printed books, would be for occasional use.

The italic style of handwriting is being taught in many schools and as it is traditional, sensible, and pleasing, it seems likely that it will establish itself in England and probably in the U.S.A. also. If one scans the horizon for a glimpse of any future style that may follow and displace it there is none. Marshall McLuhan in *The Gutenberg Galaxy* claims that we are entering a new phase of civilization with accompanying new forms of communication: the Era of the Electronic Man. There is the strange alphabet used on cheques for computers at banks and there are highly original graphic art captions of television programmes, but these are not relevant to ordinary usage in school and home.

Cest li iardins des utus. li. vij. arbre senesient les .vij. utuz dont
est liures parle. Li. arbre du melieu senesie ihucrist. souz q
croissent les utuz. Les .vij. fontaines de cest iardin sont les .vij.
dons du saint esprit qui arousent le iardin. Les .vij. puceles
qui puisent en ces .vij. fontaines sont les .vij. peticions de
la patrinostre qui empetrent les .vij. dons du saint esperit...

C. LA SOMME LE ROY. The Seven Virgins in a mystic garden, with a
hunting scene below. Illuminated by Honoré. Thirteenth century. British
Museum (Add. MS. 54180).

Formal Calligraphy Revived

Although manuscript books were eventually superseded by the invention of printing, there is often a need today for calligraphers to write formal book-hands but not only for manuscript books. Ceremonial inscriptions may be required on a special occasion: for example, a formal script would be used in writing a Royal Patent, a roll of honour, a list of names, a presentation address, a certificate, etc. Calligraphers do occasionally make transcriptions of favoured literary works in book form for bibliophiles.

Printing is for making numerous copies, often millions, but calligraphy is appropriate for the unique copy, the limited edition of one. Professional calligraphers have generally been trained as artists and designers. They will write a fine formal book-hand with care and precision and skill of hand on vellum, and will possibly decorate the inscription by illuminating. Their work will be based on tradition but will not be a slavish copy of earlier styles. Visitors to St. Clement Danes Church, in London, can see the formal scripts of many contemporary English calligraphers, for there are shrines containing ten manuscript Books of Remembrance of the Royal Air Force, and one of the American Air Force when serving in the United Kingdom.

There is a professional Society of Scribes and Illuminators which also has a lay membership.

As already mentioned, William Morris made a number of 'painted books'. These were literary works, including Icelandic sagas, written in various scripts and illuminated, preserved in libraries in England and the United States of America. Plate 37 is of a trial page now in the Bodleian Library, Oxford, where the decoration of the initial is incomplete and lacks colour. Calligraphy owes Morris a debt but a much greater one to Edward Johnston (1872–1944), whose teaching and practice have had considerable influence in this country and overseas. Figure 19 shows a part of a copy-sheet written by Johnston in the style of the tenth-century

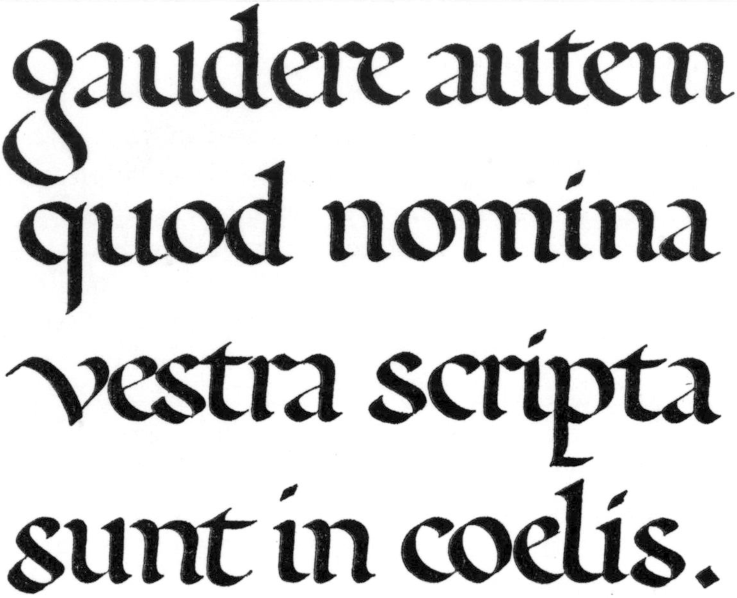

gaudere autem
quod nomina
vestra scripta
sunt in coelis.

Fig. 19. From a copy-sheet written by Edward Johnston in August 1919, in a style deriving from the *Ramsey Psalter* (see Plate 22)

hand illustrated in Plate 22, which he called the 'foundational hand'. Its relationship to roman types will be noted. This formal hand was written with a pen that had a broad point. The point was slightly oblique, the right side of the slit, as seen above the pen, being shorter than the left side. (If writing in this style left-handers would need the point to be oblique, with the left side shorter.) The letters are constructed by short strokes, pulled but never pushed against the pen's edge. For example: the letter 'o' is made of two semicircles fitted together, the first being made counter-clockwise and the second clockwise, but both by strokes moving downwards. The pen has to be lifted frequently from the vellum or paper: every

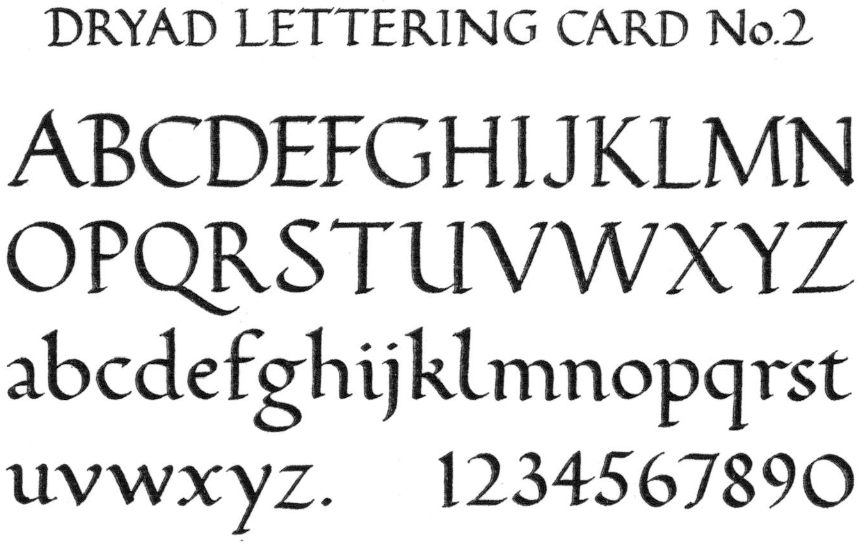

DRYAD LETTERING CARD No.2

ABCDEFGHIJKLMN
OPQRSTUVWXYZ
abcdefghijklmnopqrst
uvwxyz.   1234567890

Fig. 20. Broad pen roman alphabets and numerals
written by the author in 1935

letter has at least one pen-lift. The broad pen makes thicks, thins, and gradations naturally, and so regulated pressure, as in copperplate, is not required and there is consistency in the incidence of shading.

Speed of execution is out of place in formal calligraphy, for precision is necessary, and therefore the numerous pen-lifts and the absence of ligatures are no drawback. It will be noticed that the letters in Figure 19 end with a hair-line and the letters have a clean sharpness. The ability to write the uncomplicated letters of this script is often useful to amateurs when an italic script is not chosen for booklets, posters, labels, etc. Edward Johnston's *Writing & Illuminating, & Lettering* is the classic work on formal calligraphy. Inexpensive books giving simple instruction in this basic style are *Pen Lettering* by Ann Camp (Dryad Press) and *A Roman Script for Schools* by the author (Ginn & Co.). The alphabets of Figure 20, also by the author, are in the Johnstonian style.

D. FLEMISH BOOK OF HOURS. St. Anthony in the Desert.

Illuminated by the Master of Mary of Burgundy. Fifteenth century. Bodleian Library (Douce 219).

Illuminated Manuscripts

People down the ages, whether civilized or primitive, have decorated works which they have regarded as having importance, and in doing so have given expression to the artistic sense. Manuscript books made before the invention of printing were rare and most precious and accordingly it was natural to add ornament or illustrations or both. Because manuscripts written on vellum were bound and kept closed, they have preserved paintings from the effects of dust, light, climate, vandals, and other causes of decay. Stained glass windows and wall paintings of the Middle Ages have been vulnerable and therefore have suffered. Indeed, our heritage of the art of the Middle Ages when illuminating was so fine would be very much less but for the decoration of manuscripts. At the first sight of an illuminated manuscript book people are often surprised by its fresh quality.

The use of papyrus in remote times for writing was superseded by the durable and accessible parchment and vellum, and by this change of material the papyrus scroll was replaced eventually by the book made of folded skins, namely the *codex*. The scroll, written by Egyptians, Greeks, Romans, etc. was not without pictures. The earliest of the scrolls with illustrations that has survived, namely the Egyptian *Ramesseum Ceremonial Papyrus*, was made as long ago as the twentieth century B.C. There exist also a number of copies of the Egyptian *Book of the Dead*, and these, it is thought, may have influenced Greek illustrations. Plate 5 is from the Ani papyrus in the British Museum and comes from the Eighteenth Dynasty. A famous codex, the Vatican *Virgil*, written in rustic capitals in the fourth or fifth century A.D., has fifty pictures painted in many colours.

Another way other than by decoration of giving books an attractive appearance was by staining skins saffron, crimson, or imperial purple, and by writing on them in gold and silver.

In illuminating, the ornament which lights up the written page is made by the use of pure and permanent pigments and by metals, the metal being mostly gold: silver tarnishes. The gold was generally gold-leaf beaten to infinitesimal thinness and was made to adhere to a size (gesso) and then burnished to a glitter: a fine setting for bright colours.

The decoration of initials gave opportunities for intricate patterns. The illuminating extended from initials to fill the borders round the column of writing. Included in the ornament we may see birds, beasts, butterflies and flowers. Heraldry would show for whom the manuscript was written. Miniatures were frequently of Bible subjects and saints but also scenes of battle and chivalry, the changing seasons, the occupations of land workers and even of comic situations: e.g. a hare attacking a frightened lion with a spear.

Illuminated manuscripts were wholly made by hand, the preparation of skins, the calligraphy, the painting, and the binding, being the work of craftsmen, who by co-operation produced harmonious works of art. The scribe in (say) the eleventh century might be a monk in a monastery in Canterbury, St. Albans, Winchester or Durham, etc. serving God by his work. In contrast, a scholarly scribe in the fifteenth century may have been transcribing classical texts. A Florentine bookseller, Vespasiano di Bisticci, employed various Renaissance scribes to satisfy the demand for books. Manuscripts were made for kings and queens and other noble persons and many were intended for private worship. In the British Museum there are famous Psalters and Books of Hours and other splendid illuminated manuscripts on display.

Many Renaissance manuscripts were illuminated in a style called white vine. This style sprang from the Romanesque decoration of certain twelfth-century manuscripts which were mistakenly thought to belong to Roman antiquity, and therefore respected by the scholars (Plate 25).

The four colour plates in this book are but a limited indication of the artistic distinction of numerous illuminated manuscripts which still exist, but they do show fine miniatures and also specimens of the script in which the text of each book was written, namely Carolingian, Gothic and humanistic hands.

The 'command of hand' flourishing or 'striking' of the seventeenth-century and later writing-books, though very skilful, was as much showmanship as decoration.

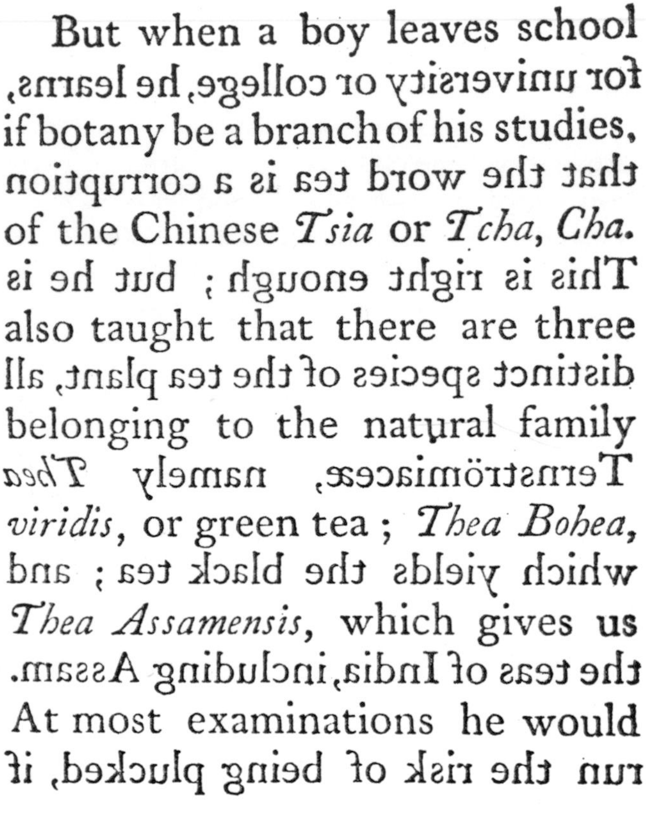

But when a boy leaves school for university or college, he learns, if botany be a branch of his studies, that the word tea is a corruption of the Chinese *Tsia* or *Tcha, Cha.* This is right enough; but he is also taught that there are three distinct species of the tea plant, all belonging to the natural family Ternströmiaceæ, namely *Thea viridis*, or green tea; *Thea Bohea*, which yields the black tea; and *Thea Assamensis*, which gives us the teas of India, including Assam. At most examinations he would run the risk of being plucked, if

Fig. 21. The *boustrophedon* system demonstrated in English. From *Are We to Read Backwards* by James Millington. 1884

Legibility

Ease in reading is helped not only by clear and simply formed letters and words, written in a traditional style, but also by orderly spacing and by regularity. Quick writing requires skill of hand and calls for care. The ability to write legibly at speed is achieved through experience and by firm intention. The writer must desire to write clearly. The motions must become practically automatic, the pen must run easily, and the letter shapes must be recognizable. A certain degree of self-discipline is essential. The greater the dash, the poorer the performance. This reads as if the handicaps against legible writing are too great, yet they are overcome and must be, for it would be nonsense to spend time and energy writing if what is written cannot be read.

Legibility, however, depends very much on what one is used to reading. When a person writes so badly that others cannot read the writing or only with great difficulty, he may not quite understand why he is being criticized, for he, himself, is used to his own writing and is therefore likely to be able to read it.

We are not used to writing, as the Chinese do, in vertical columns, starting from the right, nor to writing every other line mirrorwise and backwards as in the Greek *boustrophedon* style demonstrated in English in Figure 21. Writing cannot be deciphered if the language we use is unknown to the reader, or if the script is a non-traditional one, such as the script that gained the Bernard Shaw prize and was used in a special Penguin edition of *Androcles and the Lion*: an invented system with forty-eight characters. We should not like to have to read a book printed only in Roman capitals, although they are familiar and clear, for we are not used to reading more than a few words in capitals.

The author has heard an examiner comment: 'Why should I go to trouble to decipher the writing of a student who has not bothered to write clearly?' Men have been known to confess in a boasting way in public speeches that they find it difficult to read their own writing, as if this was amusing and socially acceptable, but, of course, they would never boast that they mumble when speaking.

A story, perhaps apocryphal, is that a painter named Loudon wrote to the first Duke of Wellington to ask permission to paint the beeches in Waterloo Park, and that the Duke replied to the Bishop of London that he had given instructions to his footman to put out the breeches he wore at Waterloo but that he could not understand His Lordship's interest in them. The Bishop expressed doubts about the Duke's sanity when at Convocation. The anecdote does not record whether Mr. Loudon ever received the permission he sought.

To write legibly is civil and logical. To write with grace is friendly and generous, and adds a little to the virtues of civilized life. Robert Bridges said that true legibility depended upon 'certainty of deciphering', which means, for example, that an n should not look like a u. A significant circumstance is that the upper part of words is of more importance to legibility than the lower part, due to movements of the eyes when reading.

Differences in Writing Styles

Because everybody is different it follows that no two persons write alike, even though the style of writing may be a common one. Consequently, we do not find it difficult to recognize the writing of our friends, for we have a good recollection of their personal styles.

The changes in writing styles down the centuries have been due to various causes. An important stage of progress for us who are right-handed was when the Greeks changed the direction of writing, and broke away from Phoenician influence, by moving from leftwards to rightwards, for this is convenient for holding the pen in the right hand and for the manner of writing. To this day, however, the writing of Hebrew and Arabic is directed leftwards.

When the Sumerians began to use clay as a writing material they scratched the surface to make the signs. This practice was not satisfactory and a natural development was when the stylus was pressed into the clay. An effect of the change was that curves were straightened. But another change, probably brought about by the dominant use of the right hand, was when the Sumerians turned the signs through 90 degrees to the left. The evolution of pictograms to signs which are no longer recognizable can also be noted in Figure 1.

In the time of the Romans, writing was on papyrus, wax tablets, and parchment, and it was also on walls and bricks. For handwriting we use paper. The professional calligrapher generally writes on vellum. The sort of writing instrument in use, which may be stylus, reed, brush, quill, metal pen, ballpoint, or pencil, and how it is held, as well as the sort of writing material, will affect the shapes of letters and words, and therefore the style of writing. Such a simple letter as 'o' has had many set shapes: round, oval, and angular.

There is another difference to be noted, which is whether the script is 'formal' or 'cursive'. The letters seen in the formal book-hands of Plates 17, 18, 22, 23, 25, 27 and 28 were made by connecting up simple strokes so that the joining is concealed. The letter 'm' of Plate 22 was made so: ꀀꀀꀀ. The pen was lifted from the vellum twice. The letter might have been written quickly and without raising the pen, to make it a cursive letter (see this letter in Plates 29, 30 and 31). The whole script will be affected by fluency, and letters may link up by running on; and in doing so speed will change the shapes of letters of the alphabets. This explains roughly why the italic letters are different from roman: e.g. the 'o' is round in roman script but oval or pointed in italic handwriting. To depart from the formal is a human and social tendency, but there is a contrary inclination to elevate the informal. The formal may become cursive and then perhaps rise to become a set hand. We may think of marching becoming easy running and conversely quick movements being disciplined and aesthetic as a part of a ballet.

Some changes appear to express or reflect the spirit of the time. In the capitals of the classic Roman inscriptions, for example, we seem to see reflected signs of the dignity and engineering skill of that great people (though some credit is due to Greek inscriptions and sculptors). The letters stand up nobly and with firm stability. The architecture and scripts of the Middle Ages are held to have some relationship to each other and to tell us something of the period and its religious spirit. Trade and conquests and the spread of religions have played a part in the changing styles. A system of writing developed in a particular region or country has often travelled to other parts. Japanese writing derives from Chinese.

Roman capitals and the small letters that go with them must now be known all over the world. A style may be revived at a later time without being a slavish imitation. The italic hand of the Italian Renaissance travelled about Europe in the sixteenth century, turned into copperplate in the seventeenth century, had extensive use in Spain in the eighteenth century, and now enjoys a revival in this country and overseas.

Fig. 22. From *Libellus valde doctus elegans*, etc., by Urban Wyss. 1549, Zurich

Motions and Shapes in Writing

If the reader looks at the hand of a person who is actually writing, what is to be seen is that fingers and thumb and probably the whole hand are moving the point of the pen on and off the paper. When one sees a trail of vapour from an aeroplane streaking across the sky it is evidence of movement but it is not serving a purpose. Conversely the movement of the pen makes a trail of ink and in laying that trail we make the shapes of letters. A copy-book shows shapes and by the shapes the pupils learn to make the correct movements. Handwriting is a system of movements, involving touch. Touch is a very personal sense. (Of course, handwriting also requires action by the mind and the eyes.)

Certain of the small letters of our alphabets are shaped principally by movements that run in opposite directions to those of some other letters. For example, the chief movement in writing *n* is clockwise, but in writing the letter *u*, which is much like an *n* upside down, it is counter-clockwise. A problem for the writing-master who designs the model of a cursive script is to find out how *n* can be saved from breaking down and becoming *u*. The italic hand may succeed in this respect where other styles fail. (The use of the words 'clockwise' and 'counter-clockwise' might be misleading in one respect. What is meant is the general direction of the stroke and not that the movements are producing a part of a circle. In making *o*, counter-clockwise, the pen comes down to make the left side and moves up on the right side, and it is much more likely to be making an oval than a circle.)

Most people have a strong sense of the perpendicular. If one bends the head over on either side the eyes tell continually what is really perpendicular. How is it then that all handwriting is not perpendicular? The reason is that the movements of the hand are not controlled by this particular ability of the eyes.

The sort of pen in use determines to some extent the shapes of letters. A pen with a definite point is held differently from an italic pen. The pen pointed to the shoulder (palm downwards) may cause writing to be flattened and spread out because of the way the hand moves sideways. The letters of the italic hand, written with the palm sideways, stand up more and are more closely spaced. The upward movements bring letters together.

In the view of the author but supported by history, the elliptical *o* goes with fluent writing and it is simpler to make an oval than a circle: there are many concepts of the shape of an oval but only one of a circle. The letter *o* should give a clue to the desirable movements and shapes of other letters. The width of the letters *abdghnpq* would be that of the *o* in an exemplar script and consequently those strokes which curve would have a relationship.

When an italic pen is used, the breadth of its edged point, whether broad, medium, or fine, should bear a relationship to the letter *o*. This relationship is called scale. If, say, the letter *s* was only three breadths high then the pen would hardly have room to move about without blobbing. A general rule is that *o* should be about five pen-breadths high. The italic pen should not be moved about in the hand: i.e. it should be held in one direction, for if the pen is turned or rolled into different positions in relation to the body the regularity of writing would be spoiled.

Writing-pressure (touch) is too individual to lay down any rule but it is desirable that it should be as light as may be. The author has noticed that calligraphers show an appreciative interest when the writing of a formal hand is seen to be by a delicate touch.

Pattern and Spacing

If one applies the right methods of penmanship and adopts a good style of script then handwriting is likely to have grace and be pleasing to the sight. A suitable pen will assist in forming good and clear shapes with regularity. The lines of writing will have pattern. A very simple pattern of two letters can be made so:

OIOIOIOIOIO OIOIOIOIOIO OIOIOIOIOIO

Because in handwriting there are many more letters of irregular sizes the pattern is much more complicated. The pattern of the characters in horizontal bands appears in Mesopotamian cuneiform and Egyptian hieratic and demotic writing.

Pattern is not confined to what is regarded as good writing, though it will certainly be found there. Even in illegible writing there may be a personal quality of rhythmical and fluent line that can be perceived to be pattern. But the pattern that will generally be agreeable is that made with a relationship to traditional alphabets, having a harmony of style, some discipline as well as freedom, and a rhythm. The finest scripts are likely to show a relationship of parts to the whole, consistency and regularity in size, proportion, slant, and spacing; or in a word 'unity'.

Pen-strokes, letters, words, and lines, may all be regarded as elements making up a larger whole, whether the whole is but a letter or a word or a line or the text. In some of the book-scripts letters stand slightly apart, being entities as well as elements of the word (Plate 28). In other formal hands letters are bunched (Plates 25 and 27). In cursive hands letters are likely to run on and link (Plate 30) and then letters seem less like entities, and words are nearer to being elements of the pattern of the line of writing and perhaps of the sentence.

Consider this pattern made by capital letters (except J and Q):

ABCDEFGHIKLMNOPRSTUVWXYZ

The letters are as if made between two horizontal lines. Words in capitals would be short bands or strips of pattern of varying length. Some of the smaller letters are also written as if between two lines: *acemnorsuvwxz*. To complete the alphabet we add letters with parts above or below the strips: *bdfghijklpqty*. The line-pattern is then more complicated, and the ascenders of *bdfhklt* and the descenders of *gjpqy* add a secondary pattern and invade and break up what would otherwise be clean blank strips between the lines of writing.

The line-pattern seemed to Romans to be so important that they often thought more of the spacing of letters than of words (Plates 13, 14, and 15). An even more regulated, patterned, and artistic Greek style called *stoichedon* is represented in Plate 12. The letters of this inscription of 408/7 B.C. were arranged in both horizontal strips and vertical columns.

There are many shapes of spaces in a page of handwriting, for what is not covered by ink remains as space. There is the background as well as the margins. Some letters have spaces wholly enclosed within them: *abdegopq*. Others have spaces partly enclosed: *chkmnuvwxyz*. And others need spaces about them—obviously *fst* and less obviously *ijlr*. In a sense, every letter has the right to as much space as it needs, but no more, so that the words can be easily recognized.

In addition to the space in and about letters are the spaces between words, the spacing of lines, and the margins. The margins are important as a means of setting off the writing. If lines are close, the ascenders and descenders may foul the writing in the line above or below. In printed books, words are often very closely spaced but still easy to read, and this points to the fact that it is certainly not essential to space written words widely.

One of the virtues of italic handwriting is that letters are fairly close together and the diagonal join allows the movement, when convenient, to go on from one letter to another and spaces them agreeably.

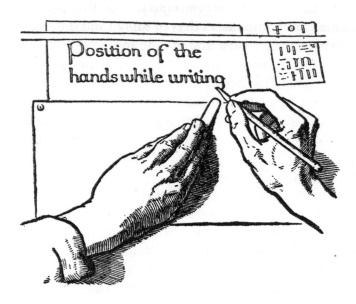

Fig. 23. Wood engraving by Noel Rooke, from *Writing & Illuminating, & Lettering,* by Edward Johnston. Sir Isaac Pitman & Sons

Pens

The pens of today could be divided into two sorts. There are those that have a slit down the middle of the point of the nib through which the ink flows and those that have a small metal ball which deposits ink from a reservoir on to the paper as the ball rotates. The latter sort, the ballpoint, is not a traditional pen and might be thought of as no more than an inky pencil. The pens with a slit, whether dip-pens or fountain-pens, are generally much superior to ballpoint pens as writing instruments, so ballpoints although popular are not recommended for good writing. However, not all dip-pens are good, for some are sharply pointed and may scratch the paper rather than run smoothly over the surface of the paper.

The triangular reed was the writing instrument for the Mesopotamian cuneiform. In Egypt and in classical Greece and Rome writing on papyrus was by the reed. A stylus of ivory, bone, or metal was a convenient tool to scratch the surface of the wax tablet. Just when the quill was introduced is not clear but a reference to the quill pen was made by St. Isidore of Seville in A.D. 624. The wing feathers used for quill pens were commonly the third or fourth of a goose, but quills from the swan, turkey, raven, and crow have often served as pens. Quills curve slightly according to whether they are taken from the right or left wing of a bird. A choice would depend upon whether the scribe preferred the quill to bend in a curve away from the hand or towards it.

Bronze pen-nibs were made by the Romans and there are a few examples in museums: one in the British Museum has a rough left-oblique point (such as left-handers might use today) and it could have been used and was suitable for writing the Roman rustic script. A Spanish calligrapher, Juan de Yciar, in his book *Arte Subtilissima* published in 1550, mentions pens of brass, iron, and steel for a 'black letter' script, but he thought that a vulture quill was best for the particular purpose.

A steel pen was made by Samuel Harrison in 1780 for Dr. Joseph Priestley, whilst a certain Mr. Wise made a split cylinder pen in 1803 which was sold for 5s. each. The metal machine-made dip-pen which is slipped into a holder was evolved early in the nineteenth century, but in slow stages. In 1809 Joseph Bramah invented a machine for cutting up quills and using the parts as pen-nibs. Some years later, tortoiseshell pen-nibs with diamond, ruby, and gold points, were patented by J. I. Hawkins and S. Mordan. Machine-made pens were probably introduced by John Mitchell about 1822, whilst James Perry has the credit for being the first maker of the steel slit-pen with a hole at the base of the slit (1830). Joseph Gillott patented an improved pen-point in 1831. About this time the quill pen began to give way to the steel pen.

The later pen-nibs were made not only from rolled sheets of the finest steel but also of other metals. Moreover, the need for pens to be easy-running then produced pens with a square or oblique point. The first italic nib, the 'Flight Commander', was made at the suggestion of the author in 1931 by Geo. W. Hughes, St. Paul's Pen Works, Birmingham, but is no longer manufactured.

Today, fountain-pens are seen everywhere and many of the manufacturers of such convenient pens have fitted them with italic nibs. The fountain-pen could be called a reservoir pen, for the barrel carries a supply of ink. A complicated reservoir pen was made in 1809 by Bartholomew Folsh but it was in December 1819 that James Henry Lewis patented a quill reservoir pen which he called 'The Caligraphic (*sic*) Fountain Pen' and which is the forerunner of the modern fountain-pen. Lewis was a writing-master and is referred to on page 56. The commercial production of the fountain-pen and its popularity began in 1880. To give the pen a long life, the nib of the fountain-pen may be of 14 carat gold or of steel but with an iridium tip. Some fountain-pens have nibs that can be replaced, some take cartridges loaded with ink, whilst others may be filled by suction or capillary attraction.

There are common things which are remarkably efficient and useful, although they are very cheap: for example, pins and buttons. The nib of the common dip-pen is one of these, for it may cost very little and yet is expected to be so efficient that it will convey a constant and consistent stream of ink down a slit as wide as a hair. This is all the more remarkable when one thinks that various forces come into play on the ink. There is not only gravity but capillary attraction and the surface tension of fluids, and there are slight movements of the split parts of the nib which, in the act of writing, squeeze or cease to squeeze the ink down the slit. It is not surprising therefore that pens must be kept clean if they are to write with a regular flow of ink.

The sort of pen used should match the style of handwriting. The copperplate hand is one where thicks, thins, and gradations of strokes, are produced by varying the pressures exerted on the nib when writing. The split parts of the pointed nib spread and come together again by the varying pressures of pen on paper. So the suitable pen for copperplate is one pointed and flexible.

A different and better sort of pen is that which does not require the skill to regulate pressures but makes thicks, thins, and gradations according to the direction of strokes and how the pen is held. This pen has a square or oblique point and has less flexibility. The point is sometimes described as a chisel-edge, and may be broad, medium, or fine. The thinnest stroke will run at right-angles to the thickest stroke and this characteristic will give a pleasing regularity to writing. Such a pen is right for the italic hand and is square-pointed unless the writer is left-handed, when a left-oblique is suitable (see page 100). There are also pens which make little or no difference in the thickness of strokes and not all of these are ballpoints.

Fig. 24. The manufacture of Chinese ink. From *Ink*, by C. Ainsworth Mitchell. Sir Isaac Pitman & Sons

Ink

To use a pen one needs ink. As with pens, a rough division can be made into two sorts: there are carbon inks and iron-gall inks.

A carbon ink is essentially a mixture of soot and gum or glue mixed with water. The soot is a fine lamp-black and might be prepared by the burning of wood or oil, but today the soot may be gas-black. The Chinese prepared such inks for use in solid sticks or blocks, cylindrical or rectangular. The writer, as he needs ink, rubs the stick of ink gently on a stone with a little water. The quality of the ink depends upon what is burnt to make the soot (pine branches were preferred), on the animal gum or glue which holds the soot together, and on the grinding. As calligraphy is valued so highly by the Chinese it follows that ink and brush was a matter of fastidious choice ('the ink supports the brush and the brush supports the ink'). An indication of extreme meticulosity is given by Professor Ch'en Chih-Mai in *Chinese Calligraphers and Their Art*. He tells of a tenth-century ink-maker Li T'ing-kuei whose formula for ink-making was 1⅓ pound of pine soot, 3 ounces of ground mother-of-pearl, 1 ounce of ground jade, 1 ounce of Baroos camphor, plus a quantity of raw lacquer. This mixture was pounded 100,000 times! The author remarks that in moments of extravagance Li T'ing-kuei also mixed into the compound such expensive materials as rhinoceros-horn, pomegranate peel, gamboge, croton-oil bean, and cinnabar. When the ink dried it was as hard as jade.

The ancient Egyptians used carbon inks for writing on papyrus. The Romans used sepia from the cuttle fish as well as the carbon inks which Pliny said were made from soot taken from the Furnaces of the Baths. Indian ink, sold in bottles, is also a carbon ink, and may have an addition of shellac to make it waterproof.

The first reference to iron-gall ink was made by Theophilus, a monk of the eleventh century, who described an ink prepared from a mixture of an extract of thorn wood with green vitriol (iron sulphate). There is reason to believe, however, that the earliest known vellum document, one of Demosthenes's *De Falso Legatione*, written in the second century A.D., and even the *Codex Siniaticus* of the fourth century A.D. were written with an iron-gall ink.

In the sixteenth-century writing-books we find recipes to make ink from galls, copperas, gum Arabic, and wine or rain water. Jean de Beauchesne's recipe is a quart of wine, two ounces of gum, three of copperas, and five of galls, but proportions differ in various recipes. Gall nuts, which contain tannin, are called in England oak apples and are caused by gall-flies. Copperas is known today as proto-sulphate of iron. Roman or green vitriol is a source also of sulphate of iron and was an alternative to copperas.

When made, an iron-gall ink would be pale but would darken when exposed to the air. In inks sold in our stationers' shops an indigo or black dye has been added. The use of indigo for ink, though described in 1770, was introduced by Dr. Henry Stephens in England in 1836.

A jet black ink may have carbon particles suspended in the fluid and these particles may clog the slit of a pen and prevent a free flow. Some inks are a mixture of the two sorts: carbon and iron-gall. Chinese ink will give the blackest writing and be the most permanent of contemporary inks but it will lie on the surface of vellum, stuck down by the gum or glue which is a component. Iron-gall inks may penetrate the surface of paper and have been known to eat into it destructively in ancient documents. The ink of ballpoint pens is slightly sticky and is nearer to the inks used in printing.

The calligrapher of today making illuminated manuscripts would use coloured inks as well as carbon black ink for his formal book-script. These coloured inks would not be red, blue, or green drawing inks sold in bottles for draughtsmen but would be prepared from pigments. He would choose pure opaque pigments of good quality that do not fade or discolour, such as those used for illuminating.

A feature pleasing to mothers is that some inks are washable. Teachers may come to like the ink-cartridges of some fountain-pens. Another comforting thought is that in England ink does not freeze in fountain-pens and ink bottles. Ink is sometimes called writing fluid, but two words are not necessarily better than one.

Paper, Vellum, and Papyrus

Paper, like pens and ink, has a long history. The oldest paper that can be dated is one made by the Chinese in A.D. 406 but the invention is traditionally attributed to an official of the Han Court, Ts'ai Lun, in A.D. 105, who is said to have used as raw materials rags, fishing-nets, and tree bark. The knowledge of the Chinese process was carried overseas to Korea and thence to Japan in the seventh century. The Arabs learned the method from Chinese prisoners taken in Samarkand in A.D. 751. The oldest known European paper bearing a date, namely A.D. 1102, is a deed of King Roger II of Sicily. In Europe paper began to be used for the less important documents, household accounts, etc. in the fourteenth century. Most paper used in England before the seventeenth century was imported, but a paper-mill was established at Stevenage by John Tate in the fifteenth century.

The forerunner of paper was papyrus, made in ancient Egypt from a reed-like plant belonging to the sedge family (*Cyperus papyrus*). This aquatic plant grew abundantly along the Nile and the Delta, but it is no longer found in Egypt, though it grows in Sicily. The earliest example of papyrus discovered so far is a blank sheet which dates back to the First Dynasty. Plate 16 shows Roman cursive writing on papyrus.

The long triangular stems of the plant bear a mop-head of thread-like growths. Six such stalks, signifying Lower Egypt, are represented in the Narmer Palette (Figure 2).

The Egyptians produced papyrus from strips of the pith of the plant arranged in two layers, with strips laid side by side and touching. The first layer was perpendicular and the second horizontal. By soaking in the Nile water and by addition possibly of glue, the two crosswise layers were united. Then the sheets were pressed, pounded, and dried in the sun, and finally the side formed by the horizontal strips was polished by shells or ivory, and rendered fit to receive writing. The sheets would be joined to make a roll, which might on occasions be over 100 feet long. Greece and Rome imported papyrus from Egypt in rolls about thirty feet long and about nine inches wide. In Imperial Rome papyrus was graded according to its quality.

Paper is made of vegetable fibres, pounded to a pulp and thinned out by water. In the eighteenth century, because of an expanding demand for paper for printing and writing, there were searches for inexpensive substitutes for cotton rags, and Dr. Jacob Schaeffer, a German clergyman, experimented with almost eighty different substances, including potatoes, beans and cabbages. Today, the best writing papers have cotton and linen rags in their composition, others have esparto grass.

Hand-made paper, though the most durable of papers, is rapidly becoming rare. A hand-made paper is difficult to tear because of the interlocking of the fibres. A slightly rough surface is corrected by hot-pressing. There are many machine-made papers which are tough and durable and have a surface smooth enough to allow the pen to run easily.

The mould for making paper by hand is like a shallow frame and is usually of mahogany. The covering of the mould through which water drains is either a laid wire sieve, for 'laid' papers, or a woven wire cloth, for 'wove' papers. When a sheet is held up to the light the sort of covering, whether laid or wove, shows through, and a laid paper reveals lines some distance apart, but a wove paper is without lines. The watermarks are designs that are nearly transparent: a design in wire is attached to the wire sieve or cloth of the mould, which will thin the fibres and show the design.

The mould is framed by the 'deckle' which limits the size of the paper and gives it its deckle edge. The deckle edges are the rough, thin, uncut edges of a sheet of hand-made paper. The 'vat-man' when making a sheet of paper dips the mould into the 'stuff' (pulp) in a vat and gives it a shake to mat the fibres. Water drains away. The sheet is removed and squeezed between felts (which explains why hand-made papers sometimes have hairs on the surface). The sheet is then dried and sized to prevent ink sinking into it, as it does in blotting-paper, and is 'finished' by being pressed.

Mass production by machine frequently develops from hand processes. The cut and shaped quill is the ancestor of the fountain-pen. Ink has the same constituents whether made in small or large quantities. The processes of paper-making by hand are imitated by complicated machines, except that sheets may be of tremendous length.

Paper has replaced prepared skins as a writing material except for such ceremonial documents as the roll of honour, the Royal Patent, and the presentation address, which may be illuminated in gold and colours. The prepared skins are known as parchment or vellum and are from lamb, calf, or kid. The skin is called vellum if from a calf, but parchment if from a lamb, but the use of the names is not always precise. The finest vellums are the small skins of calves unborn or which died at birth. The vellum-maker supplies skins ready for writing but the calligrapher dusts the surface with a resinous gum called sanderach to prevent the ink soaking in.

When writing is erased and the skin is used again for writing, the manuscript is called a palimpsest. Plate 14 shows an example.

The Teaching of Handwriting

In mediaeval times the teaching and practice of writing was principally supported by the monastic scriptoria, the notaries, the scriveners, and the Government clerks. Before the Dissolution of Monasteries the chantry priests would teach the young, but the Reformation caused their place to be taken by parish priests and others. Scribes making copies of texts became redundant by the invention of printing, but scriveners were needed for the writing of legal documents, and were organized by Guilds and recruited by apprenticeship, which usually lasted seven years.

The late Sir Hilary Jenkinson studied *The Common Paper of the Scriveners' Company of London* and found the names of 585 scriveners active between 1540 and 1628. York also was an important centre of professional handwriting. The requirements of the Government were met by clerks writing hands special to the particular office, the Royal Chancery, the Pipe Roll Office, the Exchequer, the Courts of the Common Pleas.

After the Dissolution grammar schools were founded by Edward VI and Elizabeth and by merchants and lawyers, and in these schools the pupils would be taught 'fair writing', but some grammar schools required entrants to be able to write. The petty schools were for younger pupils to learn the three R's.

A famous writing school within Christ's Hospital was founded about 1577 with a master and an usher to teach writing and the casting of accounts, but prior to this foundation John Watson, the first teacher of writing at the Hospital, received £3 6s. 8d. in 1553. A later master at the school, Jonathan Pickes, referred to on page

56, taught 200 pupils, but early in the eighteenth century, when the accomplished George Shelley was the Master, the attendance had risen to 455. (Shelley was dismissed after seventeen years of service and among the charges made against him was one of staying out late at nights.)

Plate 36 is from a thin book of examples of scripts written on vellum by John Bowack for presentation to the Earl of Oxford, Lord High Treasurer, on 31 December 1712. Bowack was writing-master at Westminster School for some years. This amusing page of the specimen book gives a display of various scripts and is a demonstration of skill, but such a mixture hardly counts as fine calligraphy. The words in the bottom panel *Capacious*, *Ocean*, *Unconfind*, and *Southern* were written in the narrow Italian Hand and are in contrast with the wider letters of the Round Hand.

The writing-master of the Tudor period would write the models to be copied, but the publication of printed writing-books lightened his task. Competition had the effect of making many copy-books into exhibitions of skill in penmanship and engraving, and often it was the decoration of writing by flourishes that was significant rather than the writing. Doubtless teaching was also done by itinerant writing-masters. Whilst boys were taught to write, read, and cast accounts, the teaching of girls to write in schools was dilatory. Martin Billingsley stated in 1618 that the ungrounded opinion of many was that writing was unnecessary for women, but he regarded it as commendable. Governesses would teach the ladies of the 'gentle' classes, but Elizabeth I and Lady Jane Gray had scholars as tutors: Roger Ascham taught Elizabeth, who did him much credit as a teacher by her penmanship when a princess (Plate 32).

The author was able to bring to notice numerous letters written from Cambridge to Elizabeth and Lord Burghley in fine italic hands. Most of the Public Orators at Tudor Cambridge University

in suis scriptis ostendit q auinum non tam

pretiosius sit plumbo .q regia potestate sit

altior ordo sacerdotalis . Stephanus qq:

papa secundus Romanum imperium

in personam magnifici Caroli a Grecis

transtulit in Germanos . Alius ite Ro.

manus Pontifex Zacharias scilicet

Regem Francorum non tam pro suis in

quitatibus .q pro eo quod tantę potestati

erat inutilis a regno deposuit : et Pipi,

num Caroli magni imperatoris patrem

in eius locum subs tituit : omnesq: Fran,

cigenas a iuramento fidelitatis absoluit .

Innocentius papa quartus Fridericum

Imperatorem suis ligatum peccatis &

30. Italic hand of an anonymous scribe. *Hadrianus: De Romanae Ecclesiae Postestate*.
About 1490. Harvard College Library.

31. Part of a Papal brief to Cardinal Wolsey. 27th August, 1519. Writing attributed to Arrighi. Public Record Office (S.P.1/19, f. 11). From *A Handwriting Manual.*

Although your hithnys letters be most ioyfull to me in abſens, yet cc
paine hit ys to you to write ʒ your grace beinge ſo great with c
your comendacyon wer ynough in my Cordes lettar . ʒ mu
your helthe with the wel likinge of the country, with my h
that your grace wiſſhed me with you til I ware wery of th
hithnys were like to be combered if I ſhulde not depart tyl
beinge with you, although hit were in the worſt ſoile in t
your preſence wolde make it pleaſant . I can not reproue
not doinge your comendacyons in his lettar for he did hit :
he had not yet I wil not coplaine on him for that he ſhalbe
giue me knolege frome time to time how his buſy childe d
I were at his birth no dowt I wolde ſe him beaton for t
put you to . Master Denny and my Lady with h
for your grace
prayeth most intirely praninge the almyghtty God t
lucky deliuerance, And my myſtres wilſeth no
most humbel thankes for her comendacions
leyſor this laſt day of Iuly .

32. Letter written by Elizabeth I when a princess to Thomas Seymour, husband of
Catherine Parr. 1548. British Museum (Cotton MS. Otho C.X.).

My very good L. I haue receaued your L. lres by Mr
Walterhouse. wherfore I thinke myself bounde to your L. bothe
for your counsell and preceptes, and I hope that my life shallbe
accordinge to your prescriptions. And since my L. and father
commened me to your L. on his deathe bed, for your L. wisdome
I hope to institute my life according to your L. preceptes. Wheras I
am appointed of the Quenes Maiesty and your L. together with my L.
Chamberlayne, to doe my L. and father the last service, I wolde be
willinge not only to do this service, but any other in my power, if that
my weake body coulde beare this iovrnay, and that all thinges weave
convenient, wherfore I most humbly her desire her Maiesty, and your
L. to pardone me. And thus wishinge your L. prosperous helthe I
bid your L. farewell. from Chartley the xviijth of Nouember. 1578.

Your L. at commaundement
as your sonne.

R. Essex

33. Letter written by the Earl of Essex when aged nine to Lord Burghley. 1575.
British Museum (Lansdowne 22, f. 200).

34. Italic hand from *A Booke Containing Divers Sortes of Hands* by Jean de Beauchesne. 1570. From *A Handwriting Manual*.

35. A page of *The Writing Schoolmaster or the Anatomy of Faire Writing* by John Davies of Hereford. 1663. From *A Book of Scripts*.

o on, *Great Sr,* Britannia claims your care,
Bow'd down and fetter'd by a *tedious War :*
She *smiles* while YOU erect Her drooping head,
And glowing *Vigour* thro each member spread.

In vain alas ! we wish for downey *Peace,*
Our *Wars* might end, but *miseries* encrease,
Did not your *Wisdom* point out remedies ;
And teach us where to seek for new *Supplies.*

The mighty views of Your *Capacious* Mind,
Vast as y. Ocean, and as Unconfind !
Extend themselves where freizing billows roul,
And Continents the Southern Seas controul.

36. Specimen scripts written by John Bowack for the Earl of Oxford. 31st December, 1712. British Museum (Harley MS. 1809).

THE most credible historians have related that Jaffier, the father of Khalid, who was called Bermuk was come of the blood of the ancient kings of Persia: Jaffier like his forefathers was in his young days a worshipper of the Fire, and priest at the fire-temple of the city of Balkh; but suddenly by the decree of the divine mercy, which suffers not the elect to abide in error, the sparks of truth were lighted up in his mind, and the glory of his state received new splendour from the refulgent graces of Islaam: with his kin and his goods he departed and came to Damascus, where as then

37. Trial page written by William Morris. About 1875. Bodleian Library (MS. Eng. Misc. d. 265, f. 6).

Come & sit under my stone pine that
murmurs so honey sweet as it bends to
the soft western breeze ; & lo this honey
dropping fountain, where I bring sweet
sleep, playing on my lonely reeds —

Thyrsis, the reveller, the keeper of the nymphs
sheep, Thyrsis who pipes on the reed like Pan,
having drunk at noon, sleeps under the shady
pine, & Love himself has taken the crook &
watches the flocks —

38. *A New Handwriting for Teachers* by Mrs. M. M. Bridges. First published 1898.
Oxford University Press. From *Renaissance Handwriting*.

were excellent penmen, and preferred the italic hand for their ceremonial letters.

In future the teaching of handwriting may be by loop-films, for this device would not only show clearly the movements making letter shapes, but relieve any teacher who found himself an inadequate and reluctant performer.

Usually a pupil learns to write by copying carefully the letters and joins of a model hand. Time and again in history, pupils have been taught by tracing the letters of the model. Beauchesne's manual for Elizabethans gives this rule:'To followe strange hand with drie penne first prove', which means one could use a pen without ink and trace the letters as if one were actually writing. By tracing, both the shapes and the movements which make them could be learnt. G. B. Palatino, an Italian calligrapher of the sixteenth century, used another method of tracing, namely to take a tablet of hard wood or copper with the alphabet cut into it. The beginner, using a stylus of tin, was intended to trace the incised letters to learn their shapes. Erasmus recommended both these methods.

Pupils are taught by teachers but they have also to teach themselves. They need to be critics of their own performances and should examine their writing to see how they can improve. This means they should know what produces good writing. A helpful way of forming taste is to study writing one believes to be good whether the examples are of the past or the present.

Richard Brinsley wrote in 1612 in *Ludus Literarius*: 'Great care should bee had withall, to make every writer to keepe even compasse in the height, greatnesse, and breadth of his letters; that no one letter stand either too high or too lowe, be over long, or over short, nor anie way too bigge, or too little, too wide or too narrow'. He might have added: 'It should be just right!' What he was aiming at was regularity.

When copying one has to go slowly but when the pupil has

passed that elementary stage then his writing will change. Running is different from walking and the movements in quick writing will not be the same as when carefully copying the model. Writing will become more personal and individual. So the model is like a sign-post: it points the way but does not take it. The model should encourage writing with a rhythm (writing is a dance of the pen) and a pattern that is not against legibility.

Writing looks sloppy if it does not have a regular slant: i.e. the straight downstrokes should have a consistent slant or be vertical, according to the style. A backslant is to be avoided. Backslant may be due to the elbow being too far from the body or to the hand as a whole not being moved enough and the movements being wholly controlled by the bending of fingers and thumb. Most good writers think any slant should be slight and in the direction of the writing. The forward slant must not be so great that the letters look to be tumbling down. Sharply angular letters brought very close together make reading difficult, whilst letters flattened and widely spread and spaced, lead to a sprawling unattractive writing.

As handwriting is by movements of the pen, certain selected drills and exercises are valuable. Of particular value in learning any Western handwriting style are drills which are short words with contrary movements, clockwise and counter-clockwise, as in *n* and *u*. A set of such words is as follows: *an, bun, can, dim, end, fun, gun, hum, inn, jam, kin, lump, mum, nun, one, pun, quince, run, sun, tan, unto, van, won, yon, zinc.*

Spacing is very important to good appearance, whether of letters or of words or of lines or of the whole writing on the sheet. Letters are more legible when they appear to be equally spaced. Margins will set off writing.

Capitals do not have to be large or too flourished or they may be too obtrusive. Everybody who receives handwriting will be pleased if it is clear and easy to read and particularly if it has a good appearance. 'Practice makes perfect' is quoted in Figure 18 but perfection is hard to attain and something less has to be accepted in fast writing for changes are inevitable and occur both from speed and personality. However, writing is a fundamental skill in making small shapes and it is by practice that skill is developed.

Fig. 25. Teaching the alphabet. Woodcut from *Ein heylsame lere und predig* by Geiler von Keiserberg. 1490. (From *Calligraphy & Palaeography*)

Left-handed Writers

Our handwriting has been developed over the centuries by the right-handed, but in spite of this handicap there are left-handed persons who write very well indeed. In *Teaching Left-handed Children*, Miss Margaret Clark has given particulars of a survey held in Scotland in 1953 which showed that among pupils of ten to eleven years of age there were more left-handed boys than girls and more in cities than in rural areas. In contrast there is the statement in the Old Testament (Judges 20, v. 16) that among the children of Benjamin 'there were seven hundred chosen men left-handed; every one could sling stones at an hair breadth, and not miss'. If this number was out of 'twenty and six thousand men that drew sword' then the proportion of left-handed was considerable.

The principal strokes made by the right-handed, whether the movements are straight or curved, are down, towards the body, and up, away from the body. The strokes away from the body are naturally to the right by the right-handed. The outward movement of the left-handed is opposite and to the left. The left-handed must therefore learn to make strokes to the right as they are made by the right-handed.

Advice to the left-handed is to place the writing-paper a little to the left of the body and to slant it so that the top left corner is higher than the top right corner. To avoid smudging, the hand should be below and not hooked above the writing. What in particular the left-handed may have difficulty with are the upward movements to the right. In the italic hand the hair-line upstrokes are most important for fluency, and the left-handed are helped to make them by using a pen with a left-oblique point. Such pens are available. Another italic pen on the market for left-handers is one where there is a bend to the left near the point and the slit is not straight but has an angle.

The left-handed writers of other styles suffer a second handicap if sharp-pointed steel nibs are used which may scratch the paper. A blunt pen which can be pushed against its point without much resistance or friction would be suitable for them. Fingers-and-thumb movements to form the letters and words are more appropriate to the left-handed than movements of the whole hand, except, of course, that the hand must move to the right as the writing progresses across the page.

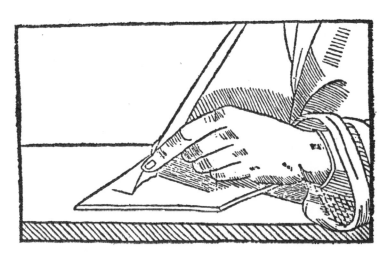

Fig. 26. From Sigismundo Fanti's *Theorica et pratica de modo scribendi*. 1514. (From *Renaissance Handwriting*)

Some Books to Consult

For the history of ancient scripts the following works are recommended and should be available in Public Libraries:

A Study of Writing by I. J. Gelb, University of Chicago Press, 1952, revised 1963.

The Alphabet: A Key to the History of Mankind by David Diringer, Hutchinson, 3rd edition 1968.

The Decipherment of Linear B by John Chadwick, Cambridge University Press, 1958, revised 1960.

Ancient Writing and Its Influence by B. L. Ullman, Harrap, 1932.

Articles on *Palaeography* by Julian Brown in *The Encyclopaedia Britannica* and by R. W. Hunt in *Chambers's Encyclopaedia*, 1966.

The Handwriting of English Documents by L. C. Hector, Edward Arnold Ltd., 1956, revised 1966.

Elizabethan Handwriting by Giles E. Dawson & L. Kennedy-Skipton, Faber & Faber Ltd., 1968.

A Newe Booke of Copies 1574. A facsimile of an Elizabethan Writing Book, edited by B. L. Wolpe, Oxford University Press, 1962.

A Book of Scripts, Penguin Books Ltd., 1949, revised 1968.

Some books relating to Renaissance Handwriting are:

The Origin & Development of Humanistic Script by B. L. Ullman, Rome, 1960.

Renaissance Handwriting: An Anthology of Italic Scripts by Alfred Fairbank and Berthold Wolpe, Faber & Faber Ltd., 1960.

The Script of Humanism by James Wardrop, Oxford University Press, 1963.

Books on formal calligraphy:

Writing & Illuminating, & Lettering by Edward Johnston, John Hogg, 1906. Numerous later editions published by Sir Isaac Pitman & Sons.

The Calligrapher's Handbook. A collection of essays by calligraphers, Faber & Faber Ltd., 1956, revised 1968.

The author has also published the following works:

A Handwriting Manual, Faber & Faber Ltd. Third revised edition 1961.

Beacon Writing Books (with Charlotte Stone and Winifred Hooper), Ginn & Co. Ltd., 1957–61.

Humanistic Script, Bodleian Library Picture Book (with R. W. Hunt), 1960.

The Italic Hand in Tudor Cambridge (with Bruce Dickins), Bowes & Bowes, 1962.

Index

Abban, 26, Pl. 3
Abecedarium, 39, Pl. 11
Accadians, 26
Acrophonic principle, 21
Adam and Eve, 19
Ahiram, King of Byblos, 36, 38
Alcuin of York, 45
Aldred, Pl. 19
Aldus Manutius, 51
Alphabets, 23, 33, 36–42, 58, 59, 62, 64
Altamira cave paintings, 19
Ammurabi, 26, Pl. 3
Ampersand, 64, 66
Ani Papyrus, 71, Pl. 5
Arabian Nights, 61, Pl. 37
Arrighi, Ludovico degli, 48, 49, 51, 61,
    Pl. 31
Ascham, Roger, 51, 96
Assyrians, 26
Athens, 39
'Atshana, 26, Pl. 3

Babylonians, 19, 26
Ballpoints, 77, 85, 90
Beauchesne, Jean de, 46, 52, 90, 97,
    Pl. 34
Behiston, Rock of, 32
Benedictional of St. Ethelwold, Pl. B
Benjamin, Tribe of, 100
Berenice, 32

Bickham, George, 54, 56
Billingsley, Martin, 96
Bittati, 26, Pl. 3
Book of Hours, Pl. D
Book of Kells, 43
Book of the Dead, 71, Pl. 5
Bouchard, 31
Bowack, John, 96, Pl. 36
Brahma, 19
Bramah, J., 86
Bridges, M. M., 61, Pl. 38
Bridges, Robert, 37, 56, 76
Brinsley, R., 97
Brushes, 30, 89
Burghley, Lord, 96, Pl. 33

Cambridge penmen, 51, 96
Camp, Ann, 70
Carpi, Ugo da, 61
Carstairs, Joseph, 56
Cennini, Pietro, 48
Chadwick, John, 32, 33
Champion, J., 19
Champollion, J. F., 31, 32, 33
Charlemagne, Emperor, 44, 45
Charles I, 53, 56
Cheke, Sir John, 51
Ch'en Chih-Mai, Professor, 29, 89
Chien Lung, Emperor, 30
Chinese radical, 22, Pl. 8

Chou bronze vessels, 29
Christ's Hospital, 56, 95
Clark, Margaret, 100
Cleopatra, 32
Command of hand, 56, 73, 96
Corbie, 45
Coster, L., 48
Croke, Richard, 51
Cumae, 39
Curlo, Giacomo, Pl. 27
Cyprus, 33

Darius the Great, 32
Davies, John, 55, Pl. 35
Dead Sea Scrolls, 35
Deciphering of ancient scripts, 31–5
Demosthenes, 90
Determinatives, 21, 22, 25, 27, Pl. 8
Differences in styles, 77–9
Direction of writing, 28, 39, 40, 77
Diringer, Dr. David, 38
Dissolution of Monasteries, 95
Dodington, Bartholomew, 51

Eadfrith, Bishop, Pl. 19
Edward VI, 51, 95
Egypt, 23, 28, 31, 85, 92, 93
Elamites, 26
Elizabeth I, 46, 51, 95, 96, Pl. 32
Erasmus, 97
Essex, Earl of, 52, Pl. 33
Etruscans, 39, 41
Evans, Sir Arthur, 33

Fanti, S., 61, 101
Folsh, B., 86
France, 43

Gelb, Professor I. J., 24, 28, 36
Germany, 43
Gestures, 20

Gillott, J., 86
Goddard, J., 53, 56
Gray, Lady Jane, 96
Greece, 20, 38, 39, 85, 93
Grotefend, G. F., 32
Gutenberg, Johann, 48

Half-uncials, 43, Pl. 18
Handwriting (see Writing)
Harrison, S., 86
Hawkins, J. I., 86
Henry VIII, 51
Heraldry, 20, 45, 72
Hermes, 19
Hewitt, Graily, 60, 61
Hierakonpolis, 27
Hittites, 26
Homonyms, 22
Honoré, Pl. C
Hughes, Geo. W., 86

Ideograms, 20, 22, 25, 27
Illuminated manuscripts, 45, 61, 67,
    71–3, 91, Pl. 24, A, B, C, D
Initial teaching alphabet, 59
Ink, 30, 89–91
Insular half-uncials, 43, Pl. 19
Ireland, 43
Italian Renaissance, 20, 47–52
Italic print-script, 58, 60
Italic types, design of, 51
Italy, 43

Jackson, J., 56, 57
Jemdet Nasr, 26, Pl. 1, 2
Jenkinson, Sir Hilary, 95
Johnston, Edward, 59, 61, 68, 70, 84
Joins in writing, 27, 47, 55, 63, 84

Kent, Duke of, 56
King Hafbur & King Siward, 61

Koch, Rudolf, 44

Language, 17, 20, 37, 75
Lascaux cave paintings, 19
La Somme le Roy, Pl. C
Left-handed writers, 100, 101
Legibility, 18, 75, 76
Leto, Pomponio, 51
Lewis, J. H., 56, 86, 87
Lindisfarne Gospels, 43, Pl. 19
Li T'ing-kuei, 89
London, Bishop of, 76
Loop-films, 97
Loudon, 76
Lucas, F., 50, 52

Majuscules, 42
Manius, 41
Marsiliana d'Alberga, 39, Pl. 11
Massey, W., 19
Master of Mary of Burgundy, Pl. D
Maurdramnus, Abbot, 45
McLuhan, Marshall, 66
Mesha, King of Moab, 38, Pl. 10
Millington, J., 74
Minuscules, 40, 42
Mitchell, C. Ainsworth, 88
Mitchell, John, 86
Moabite Stone, 38, Pl. 10
Mordan, S., 86
Morris, William, 61, 67, Pl. 37
Movements in writing, 62, 80, 81, 84,
    98, 100

Napoleon, 31
Narmer Palette, 27, 28, 92
Nebo, 19
Niccoli, N., 47, 48, Pl. 26
Numerals, 64, 66
Numerius, 41

Oracle bones, 29, Pl. 7
Oxford, Earl of, 96, Pl. 33

Palaeographers, 42, 47
Palatino, G. B., 97
Palimpsest, 94, Pl. 14
Papal briefs, 48, Pl. 31
Paper, 92–4
Papyrus, 27, 42, 71, 77, 89, 92, 93
Pattern in writing, 82–4
Pens, 30, 55, 62, 68, 77, 81, 85–8, 101
Permer, L., 33, Pl. 9
Perry, J., 86
Personality, expression of, 18
Petrarch, 47, Pl. 29
Phaistos Disc, 33, Pl. 9
Phonemes, 21
Phonetic complements, 21, 25
Phonograms, 25, 27
Pickes, J., 56, 95
Pictograms, 20, 21, 24, 77
Pitman, Sir James, 59
Pliny, 90
Plutarch, Pl. A
Poggio, B., 47, Pl. 25
Poland, 51
Porteus, Hugh Gordon, 30
Praeneste Brooch, 41
Priestley, Dr. J., 86
Printing, invention of, 42, 47, 48, 51,
    67, 71, 95
Ptolemy V, 31, 32
Punctuation marks, 64

Quill pens, 77, 85
Qumran scrolls, 35

Radicals, 22, Pl. 8
Ramesseum Ceremonial Papyrus, 71
Ramsey Psalter, 68, Pl. 22
Râs Shamrah, 37

Rawlinson, Sir H. C., 31, 32, 33
Rebus, 22
Renaissance, Italian, 47
Richardson, Marion, 59
Richmond, Duke of, 51
Roger II, King of Sicily, 92
Roman Academy, 51
Rome, 42, 85, 93
Rooke, Noel, 84
Rosetta Stone, 27, 31, 32, 34
R.A.F. *Books of Remembrance*, 67
Ruano, F., 51
Rustic capitals, 42, 43, Pl. 15

St. Clement Danes, 67
St. Ethelwold, Pl. B
St. Isodore of Seville, 85
St. Martin's Monastery, 45
Salutati, Coluccio, 47
San Vito, Bartolomeo, 48
Schaeffer, J., 93
Scrolls, 35, 71
Seals, 20, 26, Pl. 3
Senena Stele, Pl. 4
Shakespeare, W., 46
Shang-Yin Dynasty, 29
Shapes in writing, 80, 81
Shaw, George Bernard, 75
Shelley, G., 96
Shiner, 25
Simon, Professor W., 22
Simonis, A. A., Pl. 28
Slant in writing, 81, 98
Society for Italic Handwriting, 62
Society of Antiquaries, 31
Society of Scribes and Illuminators, 67
Spacing in writing, 83, 84, 98
Spain, 43, 79
Speech, 17, 22
Square capitals, 42, 43, Pl. 14
Stephens, H., 90

Stylus, 26, 77, 85
Sumer, 20, 23, 25
Syllabaries, 21

Tagliente, G. A., 61
Tate, John, 92
Teaching of handwriting, 45, 95–9
Theophilus, 90
Thoth, 19
Tophio, Antonio, 48, Pl. 29
Tours, 45
Trajan Column, Rome, 42, Pl. 13
Ts'ai Lun, 92
Ts'ang Chieh, 19

Ugarit, 37
Ullman, B. L., 43
Uncials, 43, Pl. 17
Unity in writing, 82
Ur, 25
Uruk (Warka), 25

Vatican Chancery, 48, Pl. 30, 31
Vellum, 71, 90, 94
Ventris, Michael, 31, 32, 33
Vespasiano di Bisticci, 72
Vicentino (*see* Arrighi)
Virgil, 51, 71, Pl. 14, 15

Watson, J., 95
Watts, Chi Chou, Pl. 8
Wax tablets, 42, 77, Pl. 11
Wellington, Duke of, 76
Westminster School, 96
White vine illuminating, 73, Pl. 25, 28
Wise, Marjorie, 59
Wolsey, Cardinal, 48, Pl. 31
Writing:
    Accadian, 32
    Anglo Saxon, 43, Pl. 19, 20
    Arabic, 38, 77

Writing:—cont.
Aramaic, 35
Assyrian, 26
Athenian, 39, 40, Pl. 12
Aztec, 23
Babylonian, 26
Boustrophedon, 39, 74, 75
Byblos, 36, 38
Cancellaresca, 48, Pl. 31
Carolingian, 43, 45, 73, Pl. 21-3, B
Chinese, 22, 23, 29, 30, 75, 79, Pl. 8
Copperplate, 54-7
Coptic, 32, 33
Court hands, 51, 95
Cretan, 23, 33
Cuneiform, 24, 26, 32, 37, 38, 41, 77, 82, 85, Pl. 1-3
Cursive, 21, 42, 43, 46, 78, 80, 82
Cypro-Minoan, 33
Demotic, 27, 31, 82, Pl. 6
Egyptian, 23, 27, 31, 38, 85, Pl. 4-6
Elamite, 32
Etruscan, 39, 41
Fere humanistica, 47
Formal calligraphy, 67-70, 78
Foundational hand, 68
Gothic, 45, 46, 73, 99, Pl. 24, C, D
Greek, 23, 31, 38, 39, 41, 42, 77, 78, 83, 85, Pl. 12
Hebrew, 35, 38, 77
Hieratic, 27, 82, Pl. 5
Hieroglyphic, 27, 31-3, Pl. 4
Hittite, 23
Humanistic (*see* Roman, Renaissance)

Humanistic cursive (*see* Italic)
Indus Valley, 23, 33
Italic, 47-52, 61-6, 79, 81, 84, Pl. 26, 29-34
Japanese, 79
Latin, 41-3, Pl. 14-18
Lettera antiqua, 47
Linear, 21, 32, 33
Mediaeval (*see* Gothic)
Mesopotamian, 26, 82
Persian, 32
Phoenician, 23, 36, 38, 39
Phonetic, 21, 59, 75
Pictographic, 21, 24
Primitive Semitic, 38
Print-script, 59, 60
Roman (Ancient), 23, 41, 42, 77, 78, 83, 85, 89, Pl. 13-16
Roman (Renaissance), 47, 48, Pl. 25, 27, 28, A
Secretary hand, 46, 52
Stoichedon, 40, 83, Pl. 12
Sumerian, 20, 23-6, 77
Syrian, 26, 37
Transitional, 21
Victorian, 56, 57
Writing-masters, 95, 96, Pl. 34-6
Writing-pressure, 55, 81
Wyss, Urban, 79

Yciar, Juan de, 86
Young, Dr. Thomas, 32

Ziggurat architecture, 25